Broken bodies, s
Torture and ill-treatment of women

This report is one of a series of publications issued by Amnesty International as part of its worldwide campaign against torture. Other reports issued as part of the campaign, which was launched in October 2000, include: ***Take a step to stamp out torture*** (AI Index: ACT 40/013/2000); ***Hidden scandal, secret shame — Torture and ill-treatment of children*** (AI Index: ACT 40/038/2000); ***Stopping the torture trade*** (AI Index: ACT 40/002/2001). The campaign aims to galvanize people around the world to join the struggle to end torture.

- **Take a step to stamp out torture** — join Amnesty International's campaign against torture
- Join Amnesty International and other local and international human rights organizations which fight torture
- Make a donation to support Amnesty International's work
- Tell friends and family about the campaign and ask them to join too
- Register to take action against torture at **www.stoptorture.org** and campaign online. Visitors to the website will be able to appeal on behalf of individuals at risk of torture.

Cover photo: A Romanian woman participates in a protest against domestic violence after the Romanian edition of *Playboy* magazine printed an article entitled "How to Beat Your Wife Without Leaving Marks" in April 2000. The magazine claimed it was a joke.
© Radu Sigheti/Reuters/Popperfoto

Amnesty International (AI) is a worldwide movement of people who campaign for human rights. AI works towards the observance of all human rights as enshrined in the Universal Declaration of Human Rights and other international standards. It seeks to promote the observance of the full range of human rights, which it considers to be indivisible and interdependent, through campaigning and public awareness activities, as well as through human rights education and pushing for ratification and implementation of human rights treaties.

AI's work is based on careful research and on the standards agreed by the international community. AI is a voluntary, democratic, self-governing movement with more than a million members and supporters in more than 140 countries and territories. It is funded largely by its worldwide membership and by donations from the public. No funds are sought or accepted from governments for AI's work in documenting and campaigning against human rights violations.

AI is independent of any government, political persuasion or religious creed. It does not support or oppose any government or political system, nor does it support or oppose the views of the victims whose rights it seeks to protect. It is concerned solely with the impartial protection of human rights.

AI takes action against some of the gravest violations by governments of people's civil and political rights. The focus of its campaigning against human rights violations is to:
- free all prisoners of conscience. According to AI's Statute, these are people detained for their political, religious or other conscientiously held beliefs or because of their ethnic origin, sex, colour, language, national or social origin, economic status, birth or other status – who have not used or advocated violence;
- ensure fair and prompt trials for all political prisoners;
- abolish the death penalty, torture and other ill-treatment of prisoners;
- end political killings and "disappearances";
- end abuses by armed political groups such as detention of prisoners of conscience, hostage-taking, torture and unlawful kllings;
- end grave abuses of human rights by non-state actors, such as those committed against women in the family or the community, where it can be shown that the state has failed to act with due diligence.

AI also seeks to support the protection of human rights by other activities, including its work with the United Nations (UN) and regional intergovernmental organizations, and its work for refugees, on international military, security and police relations, and on economic and cultural relations.

Broken bodies, shattered minds
Torture and ill-treatment of women

Amnesty International Publications

Please note that readers may find some of the photographs and case histories contained in this report disturbing.

First published in 2001 by
Amnesty International Publications
1 Easton Street
London WC1X 0DW
United Kingdom

www.amnesty.org

Publication date: 8 March 2001
© Copyright
Amnesty International Publications 2001
ISBN: 0 86210 296 0
AI Index: ACT 40/001/2001
Original language: English

Printed by:
The Alden Press
Osney Mead
Oxford
United Kingdom

All rights reserved. No part of this publication may be reproduced, stored in a retrieval system, or transmitted, in any form or by any means, electronic, mechanical, photocopying, recording and/or otherwise without the prior permission of the publishers.

CONTENTS

INTRODUCTION	1
Torture by private individuals	3
1: TORTURE OF WOMEN IN THE HOME AND COMMUNITY	9
Home: a place of terror	10
Women bought and sold	15
Abuses in the community	19
2: FAILURE OF THE STATE TO ENSURE WOMEN'S RIGHT TO FREEDOM FROM TORTURE	23
Failure to provide legal redress	26
Failure to investigate: gender bias in the police	30
Failure to prosecute and punish: gender bias of courts	32
Social and cultural hurdles to redress	37
3: TORTURE BY STATE AGENTS AND ARMED GROUPS	41
Torture of women in custody	42
Torture of women in armed conflict	46
4: RECOMMENDATIONS	55
Endnotes	65

© Hazir Reka/Reuters/Popperfoto

INTRODUCTION

"She was crying when she came back. She told us she had been raped by three or four soldiers. She cried for a long time. She asked us why we were lying about it because she said she knew it had happened to us too."
A woman from Suva Reka, Kosovo, 1999.

"They put a wet sponge under my neck and laid me on an electric stall. They repeatedly exposed me to electric shocks over several hours... Afterwards they put me on another table... And they brought a truncheon. They told me 'Kneel down'. And they slowly inserted the truncheon into my anus. Suddenly, they pushed me and forced me to sit on the truncheon. I started to bleed. ...one of them came, climbed on me and raped me."
The Turkish police officers alleged to have tortured Zeynep Avci in late 1996 were not prosecuted.

When she was 15, Ms G's parents traded her to a neighbour as a wife, in exchange for his assistance in paying off the mortgage on their farm. Her husband routinely raped and beat her, resulting in injuries which required hospitalization. Ms G went to the police twice for protection, but was told they could do nothing because the problem was personal. When she was 20, she ran away with her two children, but her parents and husband found her, and her mother held her down while her husband beat her with a stick. He took the children, whom she has not seen since. Ms G fled to the USA and applied for asylum.
An immigration judge told Ms G's attorney in 2000 that he intended to order her to be deported back to El Salvador.

A woman in a village in a war-torn European country, a young Kurdish woman in Turkish police custody, a battered mother of two from Central America seeking asylum in the USA. On the surface, little links these three women other than their gender and their suffering: they come from different

An ethnic Albanian woman from Kosovo in the Stenkovec refugee camp in Macedonia. Some 850,000 ethnic Albanians, predominantly women and children, fled or were forcibly expelled from Kosovo between March and June 1999. They were fleeing gross human rights violations including arbitrary detention, "disappearances", torture (including rape) and killings.

countries and dissimilar communities, and the men who assaulted them have very different backgrounds.

What connects these three cases is that all three women have been the victims of torture. All three women have had to contend not only with violent physical abuses, but also with official silence or indifference. In all three cases, the men who abused them committed their crimes with impunity. In all three cases, the state failed to take the basic steps needed to protect women from physical and sexual abuse. The state therefore shares responsibility for the suffering these women have endured, whether the perpetrator was a soldier, a police officer or a violent husband.

Torture of women is rooted in a global culture which denies women equal rights with men, and which legitimizes the violent appropriation of women's bodies for individual gratification or political ends. Women's groups and other human rights activists around the globe have fought courageously in recent decades to prevent and combat abuses and to win greater equality for women. In many countries they have achieved enormous advances, and internationally they have altered the terms of the human rights debate irrevocably. However, for all the gains that women around the world have made in asserting their rights, women worldwide still earn less than men, own less property than men, and have less access to education, employment and health care. Pervasive discrimination continues to deny women full political and economic equality with men.

Violence against women[1] feeds off this discrimination and serves to reinforce it. When women are abused in custody, when they are raped by armed forces as "spoils of war", when they are terrorized by violence in the home, unequal power relations between men and women are both manifested and enforced. Violence against women is compounded by discrimination on grounds of race, ethnicity, sexual orientation, social status, class and age. Such multiple discrimination further restricts women's choices, increases their vulnerability to violence and makes it even harder for them to gain redress.

Sometimes the perpetrators of these acts of violence are state officials, such as police, prison guards or soldiers. Sometimes they are members of armed groups fighting against the government. However, much of the violence faced by women in everyday life is at the hands of the people with whom they share their lives, whether as members of their family, of their community or as their employers. There is an unbroken spectrum of violence that women face at the hands of men who exert control over them.

Amnesty International (AI) has documented countless cases of women being tortured in custody. In its coverage of armed conflicts, it has reported the systematic use of sexual violence as a weapon of war. Since 1997, it has investigated abuses committed by private individuals.[2] AI applies a human rights framework to combat violence against women and insists that under international human rights law, states have a responsibility to protect women from violence, whether the acts are committed by state officials, at the instigation of state officials or by private individuals.[3] This report explores the circumstances in which violence against women, whether in custody or at home, constitutes torture. As part of its campaign for an end to torture, AI holds states accountable for all acts of torture of women, whatever the context in which they are committed and whoever is the perpetrator.

Torture by private individuals

International human rights treaties not only regulate the conduct of states and set limits on the exercise of state power, they also require states to take action to prevent abuses of human rights. States have a duty under international law to take positive measures to prohibit and prevent torture and to respond to instances of torture, regardless of where the torture takes place and whether the perpetrator is an agent of the state or a private individual.

The International Covenant on Civil and Political Rights requires states to "ensure" freedom from torture or ill-treatment. The UN Human Rights Committee, the expert body that monitors implementation of the Covenant, has stated: "It is the duty of the State party to afford everyone protection through legislative and other measures as may be necessary against the acts prohibited by article 7 [torture and ill-treatment], whether inflicted by people acting in their official

> **UN Convention against Torture**
> Article 1: "For the purposes of this Convention, the term 'torture' means any act by which severe pain or suffering, whether physical or mental, is intentionally inflicted on a person for such purposes as obtaining from him or a third person information or a confession, punishing him for an act he or a third person has committed or is suspected of having committed, or intimidating or coercing him or a third person, or for any reason based on discrimination of any kind, when such pain or suffering is inflicted by or at the instigation of or with the consent or acquiescence of a public official or other person acting in an official capacity. It does not include pain or suffering arising only from, inherent in or incidental to lawful sanctions."

capacity, outside their official capacity or in a private capacity".4

The UN Convention against Torture establishes the responsibility of the state for acts of torture inflicted "at the instigation of or with the consent or acquiescence of a public official".

The European Court of Human Rights has affirmed that states are required to take measures to ensure that individuals are not subjected to torture or ill-treatment, including by private individuals. In 1998, the Court found that the United Kingdom had violated Article 3 of

Protesters against domestic violence gather outside the Statehouse in Boston, USA, in October 2000. Their signs bear the names of women who the demonstrators say died as a result of domestic violence in the previous year.

the European Convention on Human Rights prohibiting torture and ill-treatment, because its domestic law did not provide adequate protection to a nine-year-old boy beaten with a cane by his stepfather.[5]

Human rights treaties are "living instruments", which evolve and develop over time. Decisions by the intergovernmental bodies which monitor states' compliance with international treaties, as well as by national courts, continually refine and develop the interpretation of what constitutes torture.[6] Largely thanks to the efforts of the worldwide women's movement, there is wider understanding that torture includes acts of violence by private individuals in certain circumstances.

Acts of violence against women constitute torture for which the state is accountable when they are of the nature and severity envisaged by the concept of torture in international standards and the state has failed to fulfil its obligation to provide effective protection.

Severity of the harm

The severity of the harm inflicted upon women by private individuals can be as damaging as that inflicted on women who are tortured by agents of the state. The long-term effects of repeated battering in the home are physically and psychologically devastating. Women are traumatized and injured by rape, wherever the crime takes place. The medical consequences include psychological trauma, wounds, unwanted pregnancies, infertility and life-threatening diseases.

Intentionally inflicted

Many abuses in the family or community are intentionally inflicted. In addition, such abuses are often inflicted for similar reasons to torture in custody. Torture in custody is often used not only to extract confessions but also to instil profound dread into victims, to break their will, to punish them and to demonstrate the power of the perpetrators. Similar purposes characterize acts of torture in the family or the community. The perpetrators may seek to intimidate women into obedience or to punish women for allegedly bringing shame on relatives by their disobedience.

State responsibility

The perpetrators of violence against women in the home and community are private individuals, but this does not necessarily mean that the state escapes responsibility for their actions.

Under international law, the state has clear responsibility for human rights abuses committed by non-state actors — people and organizations acting outside the state and its organs. Internationally, the state is accountable in a number of specific ways. It can be deemed responsible for carrying out the human rights violation because of a connection with the non-state actors, or it can be responsible for its failures to take reasonable steps to prevent or respond to an abuse. The way in which the state is responsible is categorized in different ways. These include complicity, consent or acquiescence, and failure to exercise due diligence and to provide equal protection in preventing and punishing such abuses by private individuals. In all these circumstances, the state is allowing violence against women to continue, and in this report the term "failure of state protection" is used to cover complicity, consent, acquiescence and lack of due diligence.

> Kajal Khidr, who was pregnant at the time, was detained by her husband's relatives in 1996 in Iraqi Kurdistan. They accused her of extra-marital sex, cut off her nose, and said they would kill her after her child was born. She escaped following hospital treatment and found protection in a women's refuge in the city of Sulaimaniya. With the help of human rights activists Kajal Khidr escaped abroad and was granted asylum.

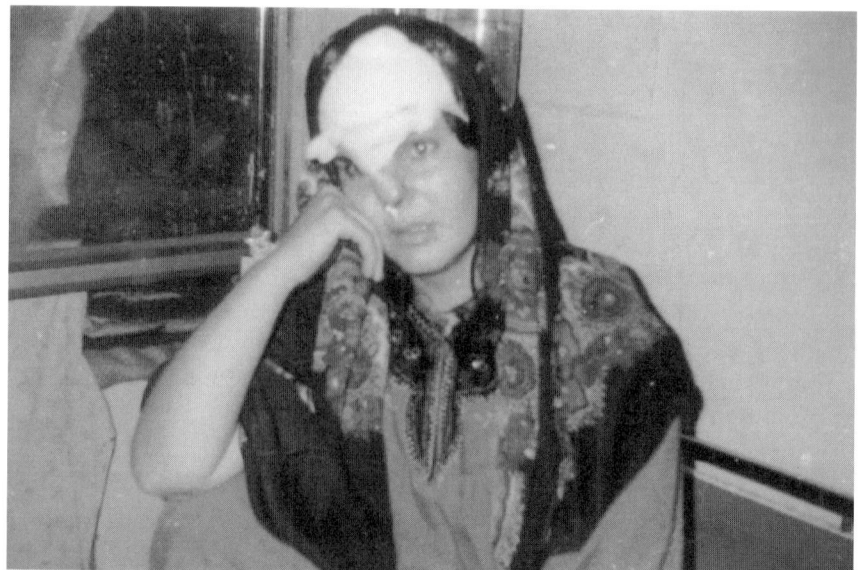

Due diligence

The concept of due diligence describes the threshold of effort which a state must undertake to fulfil its responsibility to protect individuals from abuses of their rights. The Special Rapporteur on violence against women has held that " a State can be held complicit where it fails systematically to provide protection from private actors who deprive any person of his/her human rights."[7] Due diligence includes taking effective steps to prevent abuses, to investigate them when they occur, to prosecute the alleged perpetrator and bring them to justice in fair proceedings, and to ensure adequate reparation, including compensation and redress. It also means ensuring that justice is dispensed without discrimination of any kind.

The standard of due diligence was articulated and applied by a regional human rights court, the Inter-American Court of Human Rights. The Court stated: "An illegal act which violates human rights and which is initially not directly imputable to a State (for example, because it is the act of a private person or because the person responsible has not been identified) can lead to international responsibility of the State, not because of the act itself, but because of the lack of due diligence to prevent the violation or to respond to it as required by the Convention [American Convention on Human Rights]."[8]

The Court stated: "The State has a legal duty to take reasonable steps to prevent human rights violations and to use the means at its disposal to carry out a serious investigation of violations committed within its jurisdiction, to identify those responsible, to impose the appropriate punishment and to ensure the victim adequate compensation."[9] The Court pointed out that a single violation of human rights or one ineffective investigation does not establish a state's lack of due diligence.

State inaction can be seen in a range of different areas. These include inadequate preventive measures; police indifference to abuses; failure to define abuses as criminal offences; gender bias in the court system; and legal procedures which hamper fair criminal prosecution. Many women victims of violence find access to legal redress and reparations difficult, if not impossible. Impunity and indifference habitually surround many acts of violence against women.

Focusing on when the state fails to protect people from harm by others, and how it can be held to share responsibility for the harm, does not ignore the original abuser's responsibility. In every case, the direct perpetrators must be fairly tried and punished for their crimes.

> AI considers that acts of violence against women in the home or the community constitute torture for which the state is accountable when they are of the nature and severity envisaged by the concept of torture in international standards and the state has failed to fulfil its obligation to provide effective protection.

1: Torture of women in the home and community

Dalit women at a public hearing on violence against members of the *dalit* community held in Chennai, India, in 1998. (*Dalit* literally means "broken people", a term used to describe members of the Scheduled Castes, formerly known as "untouchables.") *Dalits* are a disadvantaged social group, and violence against *dalit* women is common.

"A tooth knocked out in a fit of anger, a leg broken in a vicious attack, a life snuffed out amid screams of terror in the dead of night. The all too familiar landscape of domestic violence in Kenya is dotted with tales of woe; with teeming numbers of maimed and destitute victims; with homeless children straying into crime; with wounded hearts crying out in shame. We're still counting the dead; for there is a victim succumbing to a fatal blow every single day." This is the summary of an article which won its author a coveted journalist's award.[10] Stories about abuses of women may win plaudits, but combating such abuses takes time, resources, imagination, political will — and an unswerving commitment to women's rights.

States have a duty to ensure that no one is subjected to torture or ill-treatment, whether committed by official state agents or by private individuals. Far from providing adequate protection to women, states all around the world have connived in these abuses, have covered them up, have acquiesced in them and have allowed them to continue unchecked.

Every year, violence in the home and the community devastates the lives of millions of women. UN Secretary-General Kofi Annan acknowledged in June 2000 that since the Fourth World Conference on Women five years earlier, violence against women had been made illegal almost everywhere but such violence had in fact increased.[11]

Violence against women is rooted in discrimination, and reinforces discrimination. The failure of a state to ensure that women have equal opportunities for education, shelter, food, employment and access to formal state power is another facet of the state's responsibility for abuses of women.[12] Continued discrimination against women contributes to their inadequate participation in decision-making. Making women's voices heard at all levels of government is essential to enable women to contribute to policies that counter abuses and combat discrimination.

Poor and socially marginalized women are particularly liable to torture and ill-treatment. In many cases, racist and sexist policies and practices compound the violence they experience and increase their vulnerability to further violence. Social and cultural norms which deny women equal rights with men also render women more vulnerable to physical, sexual and mental abuse. The common thread is discrimination against women, the denial of basic human rights to individuals simply because they are women.

Home: a place of terror

"**Without exception, women's greatest risk of violence comes not from 'stranger danger' but from the men they know, often male family members or husbands ... What is striking is how similar the problem is around the world**". This is the conclusion of a major recent study.[13] Violence in the home is a truly global phenomenon. The figures may vary in different countries but the suffering and its causes are similar around the world.

Domestic violence as torture or ill-treatment

"K", from the Democratic Republic of the Congo (formerly Zaire), was married to an army officer who regularly tortured her by beating and kicking her, often in front of their children. He repeatedly raped her, infecting her with sexually transmitted diseases. He also frequently threatened to kill her with a gun. During one incident, he knocked out a tooth, dislocated her jaw

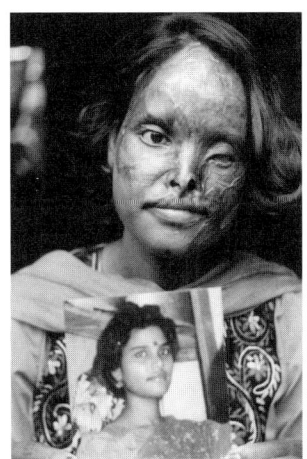

Bina, from Bangladesh, holds a picture of herself before she had acid thrown in her face. She is now in the USA, runs for her college athletics team, and is awaiting plastic surgery.

Some 200 cases of acid-throwing are believed to occur every year in Bangladesh, mostly committed by jilted suitors and abusive husbands. The disfigurement caused is permanent and extremely painful. Many women lose their eyesight and the acid often permanently joins chin to chest or lips to nose. The pain and distress are compounded by the (often justified) fear of rejection by husband, family and community.

and punched her in the eye so hard that she required stitches and had continued problems with her nose, neck, head, spinal column, hip and foot. "K", who finally sought asylum in the USA, said it was futile to approach the police, not only because of her husband's connections to the ruling family but also because "women are nothing in the Congo". A US immigration judge characterized the abuses she had suffered as "atrocities" but denied her application for asylum, a decision upheld by the immigration appeal court.

In the past, violence against women in the home was viewed as a private matter, not an issue of civil and political rights. Today, the international community has explicitly recognized violence against women as a human rights issue involving state responsibility.

According to World Bank figures, at least 20 per cent of women around the world have been physically abused or sexually assaulted. Official reports in the USA say that a woman is battered every 15 seconds and 700,000 are raped every year. In India, studies have found that more than 40 per cent of married women reported being kicked, slapped or sexually abused for reasons such as their husbands' dissatisfaction with their cooking or cleaning, jealousy, and a variety of other motives.[14] At least 60 women were killed in domestic violence in Kenya in 1998-99, and 35 per cent of women in Egypt reported being beaten by their husbands.[15] For millions of women the home is not a haven but a place of terror.

Violence in the home is a violation of women's right to physical integrity. It can go on for years and may escalate over time. It can cause serious long-term health problems beyond the immediate injury; the physical and psychological impact appears to be cumulative and may persist even when violence stops. Violence in the home is intimidating, degrading and humiliating — it destroys self-esteem.

Violence in the home takes many forms. Dowry-related violence has recently received attention, thanks largely to the efforts of women's groups in Asia. Although no one knows the number of Indian women beaten, burned or otherwise physically abused in connection with dowry demands, some idea of the scale is indicated by the Indian government's statement that 6,929 dowry deaths were reported in 1998.

Women of every class, race, religion and age suffer violence at the hands of men with whom they share their lives. But some groups of women are especially vulnerable to violence in the home — these include domestic workers and women in forced marriages. If the state fails to take action to prevent, prosecute and punish these acts, this violence can constitute torture.

Torture and ill-treatment of domestic workers

Domestic workers, many of whom are foreign nationals, are frequently ill-treated by their employers. Women who have entered the country illegally, who have been trafficked or robbed of their papers, are even more susceptible to abuse and unlikely to obtain legal redress.

In Saudi Arabia, women domestic workers, most of whom come from South and Southeast Asia, are generally strictly isolated from the rest of society. Their employers usually confiscate their passports and confine them to the house where they work. They may be transferred to other employers without their consent. The protection afforded to other workers under Saudi Arabian labour laws does not apply to them. They cannot even leave the house to get help, as women in Saudi Arabia are not permitted to go out in public unless accompanied by a *mahram* — a male relative to whom marriage would not be permitted.

Nasiroh, a young Indonesian woman, went to Saudi Arabia in 1993 as a domestic worker.[16] She told AI that she was sexually abused by her employer, falsely accused of his murder and then tortured and sexually abused by police officers during two years' incommunicado detention. Officials from her embassy did not visit her once. Her trial was so cursory that she did not know she had been convicted. She still has no idea for what "crime" she was imprisoned for five years.

Abuse of domestic workers is not restricted to any one part of the world. Many domestic workers in the USA, especially those without legal status, live in conditions of forced labour, have their passports confiscated and suffer a variety of abuses. In the UK, more than 2,000 cases of abuse of female domestic workers, including physical assault and sexual violence, were documented between 1987 and 1998. Most of the women were foreign nationals whose immigration status did not give them the right to change employment. If they left their employer, they became "illegal immigrants".[17]

Nasiroh, an Indonesian national working in Saudi Arabia, was abused by both her employer and the police. She was unaware that she had been convicted of any offence, but spent five years in prison in Saudi Arabia.

Torture and ill-treatment in forced marriages

In some countries, women and girls suffer torture and ill-treatment after being forced, usually by their parents, into marriage. Forced marriage is in itself a violation of human rights, and it provides a context for sexual intercourse without consent, and physical violence.

Forced marriage violates the requirement of free and full consent by both parties inherent in the right to marry. The Universal Declaration of Human Rights states: "Marriage shall be entered into only with the free and full consent of the intending spouses". Forced marriages also violate further rights of women, including the right to freedom from discrimination, to personal liberty and security, and to freedom from slavery-like practices.[18] Marriages of young girls, who are not in a position to give informed consent to sexual relations, violate the UN Convention on the Rights of the Child which proclaims the right to be free from sexual abuse. Such early marriages expose young girls, sometimes pre-pubescent and generally immature, to non-consensual sexual relations which amount to child sexual abuse.[19]

Forced marriages — marriages without the consent of one or both partners — occur in diverse cultures and traditions. Usually it is the woman's consent which is not sought or whose dissent is ignored. In many parts of the world, parents negotiate a marriage with the parents of the prospective husband, ignoring the wishes of their daughter.

In large parts of Pakistan, fathers of both prospective spouses negotiate a marriage "deal" which includes payment of a "bride price". This practice bears many similarities to slavery. Pakistani men may be forced into an arranged marriage, but they can marry a second wife of their own choice, and can easily divorce an enforced wife. If young women try to resist their parents' decisions, they are often subjected to physical abuse.

For example, Humaira Khokar from Okara, Punjab province, married the man of her choice instead of the man her father had chosen. She was locked up in her parents' house, and when she escaped to join her husband, was hunted down and abducted from Karachi airport as the couple tried to leave Pakistan. She was repeatedly threatened with death and probably owes her life to the timely intervention of local women activists. Her husband reported that at Karachi airport his wife's relatives "ripped off my wife's veil and dragged her by the hair through the hall, they beat all of us. There were many people witnessing our ordeal but everyone was scared and did not dare help."[20]

Young women of South Asian origin who are born and brought up in a western country and often hold dual nationality have been abducted by family members and forcibly married to men they neither know nor agree to marry in the country of their parents' origin.[21] Media reports speak of up to 1,000 such cases among British Asian women each year. Typically, the young women are lured or forced to travel to South Asia on the pretext of seeing an ailing relative or a holiday. On arrival, their passports are usually confiscated and they are effectively imprisoned in the family home until their wedding.

Torture and ill-treatment in the name of 'honour'

"We, the women, work in the fields all day long, bear the heat and sun, sweat and toil and tremble all day long, not knowing who may cast a look upon us. We stand accused and condemned to be declared a kari *[literally a*

black woman, suspected of illicit sexual relations] and murdered."[22] **Testimony of a young Pakistani girl.**

Girls and women of all ages are assaulted in the name of honour in countries in every region of the world. They are accused of bringing shame on their families and their community by their behaviour. This can range from chatting with a male neighbour to sexual relations outside marriage. It can involve something a man has done to them against their wishes. The mere perception that a woman has contravened the code of sexual behaviour damages honour. The regime of honour is unforgiving: women on whom suspicion has fallen are not given an opportunity to defend themselves, and family members have no socially acceptable alternative but to remove the stain on their honour by attacking the woman.

The treatment of women as commodities — the property of male relatives — contributes to this form of violence against women. Ownership rights are at stake in conflict settlements involving handing over women, and when the chastity of women is called into question. In honour crimes, the woman victim is seen as the guilty party, the man who "owned" her as the victim who has suffered loss of honour. Consequently he is the aggrieved person with whom the sympathies of the community lie.

So-called "honour crimes", including torture and killings, are reported from several countries including Iraq, Jordan and Turkey. While perpetrators are usually convinced of the righteousness of their actions, social approval is slowly diminishing in Jordan, possibly because of the impact of the royal family's public and outspoken criticism of such crimes.

Women bought and sold

Abuses of women's right to freedom from torture rarely occur in isolation. The denial of the right to equality, often compounded by discrimination on grounds such as race, ethnicity or class, facilitates further abuses. Poverty, lack of education and health inequalities involve the denial of basic social and economic rights and also restrict women's access to redress. Women who have been bought and sold — whether trafficked women or bonded labourers — are rarely offered redress and support if they seek help, but often face further punishment if they dare to speak out.

Torture and ill-treatment of trafficked women

"I had a nervous breakdown. I wanted to escape from this place and asked a client to help me. He turned out to be one of them and I was beaten up by the owners. There was nowhere to run — there were bars on the windows and bodyguards all the time, day and night."

Valentina, a 27-year-old Ukrainian psychologist and a social worker, arrived in Israel in August 1998. She believed she was going to work as a company representative. Her money, passport and return ticket were taken from her and she was taken to an apartment where she was held for two months and forced to work as a prostitute.

"The conditions were terrible. One girl was kept to work in the basement for eight months. It was damp there and she got tuberculosis as a result. Most of the girls had different diseases — venereal and others related to their reproductive organs. I do not wish even to my enemies to go through what we went through."

Valentina eventually succeeded in escaping but was arrested in March 1999 for not having proper documents or a visa. She was afraid to testify against the man who sold her to the brothel owners because he knew the whereabouts of her family in Ukraine. When AI interviewed her, Valentina did not know how long the Israeli authorities intended to hold her or when she would be allowed to go home.

Trafficking in human beings is the third largest source of profit for international organized crime, after drugs and arms, with a yearly turnover of billions of dollars. The UN believes that four million people are trafficked every year. Most governments are only now beginning to take note of the issue, more often than not from a law and order rather than from a human rights perspective.

The scale of the problem is huge. A US Department of State report released in 2000 stated that between 45,000 and 50,000 women and children were trafficked into the USA each year. A nationwide crackdown on trafficking in China led to the reported rescue of more than 10,000 women and children within the first month. Officials said that the women were to be sold into prostitution in the south of the country or into forced marriage with farmers.[23]

Women are recruited on false pretences, coerced, transported, bought and sold for a range of exploitative purposes. Among these are forced labour, including forced domestic labour, and sexual exploitation, including sex tourism and forced marriage. Some are completely duped about the nature of the work they will be doing; some are told half-truths about the work and are then forced to carry it out; some are aware of the nature of the work but not of the conditions in which they will perform it, and see no viable economic alternative.

Trafficked women are subjected to a wide range of human rights abuses, many of which constitute torture or ill-treatment. Women who are trafficked for sexual exploitation are often sexually abused and raped to break them mentally and emotionally, in order to force them into sex work. Many are beaten and raped to punish them for trying to escape or for refusing to have sex with customers. Despite the risks of HIV/AIDS, women are punished for refusing unprotected sex.

As well as physical violence, trafficked women suffer other abuses, including unlawful confinement, confiscation of identity papers, and even enslavement. These abuses are compounded by the treatment trafficked women receive from state officials, who treat them as criminals rather than victims.

Trafficking is prohibited under several international human rights treaties including the the UN Supplementary Convention on the Abolition of Slavery, the Slave Trade, and Institutions and Practices Similar to Slavery. The UN Convention on the Elimination of All Forms of Discrimination against Women provides: "States Parties shall take all appropriate measures, including legislation, to suppress all forms of traffic in women and exploitation of prostitution of women." A new Convention against Transnational Organized Crime, which was adopted by the UN General Assembly in November 2000, includes a Protocol to Prevent, Suppress and Punish Trafficking in Persons, Especially Women and Children.

Torture and ill-treatment of women in debt bondage

Millions of people live in debt bondage all over the world, working unwaged to pay off loans from landlords or employers. Whole families come into bondage when they need a loan because of sickness, failed crops or costly family commitments like weddings. Bonded families are forced to live where they work and only the head of the family is paid. The wage does not cover the living expenses of the whole family, forcing the family to take up further loans. Most bonded labourers are illiterate and innumerate, and cannot prove that they have repaid the loan, sometimes many times over, by their own work and that of their wives and children. In some cases, bonded labourers are bought and sold — parts of families are sold to others without regard to family ties. Debt bondage has been recognized as a practice similar to slavery.[24]

Bonded labourers are held in bondage by unlawful confinement, abuses and threats. Many bonded labourers are locked up by their "owners" after work, sometimes in chains, to prevent them escaping or to punish them.

Landlords and their managers routinely summon women and girls and insist on having sex.

Women bonded labourers

© Shakil Pathan/Anti-Slavery International

A woman bonded labourer from Pakistan told AI: *"All of us women were gang-raped. What could we do if they called us to come out? Sometimes they did not even bother but took us right in front of our husbands and children. They did not care about our shame. ...they also raped some of our girls, some only 10, 11 years old... Several of us bore children as a result of such rapes. ... Our husbands could do nothing, they were locked up or sent away if they disobeyed."*

Abuses in the community

Women whose lives do not conform to society's expectations are often the victims not only of ostracism but also of violent treatment. The UN Special Rapporteur on violence against women has stated that: *"In most communities, the option available to women for sexual activity is confined to marriage with a man from the same community. Women who choose options which are disapproved of by the community, whether to have a sexual relationship with a man in a non-marital relationship, to have such a relationship outside of ethnic, religious or class communities, or to live out their sexuality in ways other than heterosexuality, are often subjected to violence and degrading treatment."*[25]

The link between controlling women's sexuality and violence against women goes beyond punishing those who transgress accepted norms. Millions of girls have been subjected to the trauma and pain of female genital mutilation.

Female genital mutilation

Female genital mutilation (FGM) refers to the removal of part, or all, of the female genitalia. It involves the excision of the clitoris, and sometimes the cutting out or stitching together of the inner or outer labia, leaving just a small opening for urine and menstrual blood. The operation sometimes results in excessive bleeding, infection, trauma and pain. It often leads to later difficulties in intercourse and childbirth. The practice is linked in many countries with rites of passage for women. It is reported to be prevalent in countries including Burkina Faso,

Chad, Djibouti, Egypt, Eritrea, Gambia, Ethiopia, Mali, Nigeria, Sierra Leone, Somalia and parts of Sudan and is also reported from some communities in South Asia. According to the World Health Organization, two million girls each year are put through the terrifying and painful experience. Worldwide some 100 to 140 million women have undergone some form of FGM.

The practice is opposed by women's groups in Africa and elsewhere as a violation of the right to physical integrity. Opponents consider FGM a particularly violent form of controlling the status and sexuality of women. In August 2000, the UN Sub-Commission on the Promotion and Protection of Human Rights affirmed that governments should mobilize public opinion "in particular through education, information and training, in order to achieve the total eradication of these practices".[26]

Making FGM a criminal offence has raised problems, driving the practice underground, where it is carried out by unskilled

One of hundreds of women marching through Nairobi, Kenya, to campaign against violence against women holds a placard reading "Thanks, mum, for not circumcising me".

practitioners, and deterring women from seeking medical help because of the fear of prosecution. In Tanzania, where at least 85 per cent of women in rural areas have undergone FGM, an act passed in 1998 made it a criminal offence to carry out FGM on women under the age of 18, but few other steps were taken to curb the practice. Human rights activists have reported girls being taken across the border to Kenya to have the mutilation performed. One Tanzanian activist said, "the practice is escalating despite concerted efforts to curb it ... because the practice is strongly supported by the elders and young people who fear non-acceptance in their community of family and peers."[27] Several ethnic groups, such as the Maasai and the Chagga, consider FGM an important heritage necessary in order to be accepted among ancestral spirits after death. One human rights group is promoting an experiment among the Maasai in which the initiation ceremonies are maintained but without the physical mutilation.

In Mali, where about 80 per cent of girls and women reportedly undergo FGM, activists working towards eradication have received death threats. Fatoumata Sire said: "I have had death threats against me, there have been attempts to burn down my house, I have been in three car crashes and every day, Islamic radio here in Bamako broadcast curses against me."[28]

Many campaigners in Africa now focus their attention not on persuading men about the abusive nature of FGM, but on convincing the respected women practitioners of the health risks and harmfulness of the practice. Integral to this work is the provision of alternative income generating activities of similar social status. Persuasion has led to a significant reduction of the practice in Guinea, where after 14 years of campaigning by women activists, hundreds of women who had traditionally performed the operation handed in their special ceremonial knives in August 2000.

LESBIENNES VICTIMES DE BRUTALITES POLICIERES, D'ASSASSINATS POLITIQUES, DE DISPARITIONS

2: Failure of the state to ensure women's right to freedom from torture

From the moment Rodi Adalí Alvorada Peña married a Guatemalan army officer at the age of 16, she was subjected to intensive abuse, and all her efforts to get help were unsuccessful. Her husband raped her repeatedly, attempted to abort their second child by kicking her in the spine, dislocated her jaw, tried to cut off her hands with a machete, kicked her in the vagina and used her head to break windows. He terrified her by bragging about his power to kill innocent civilians with impunity. Even though many of the attacks took place in public, police failed to help her in any way. After she made out a complaint, her husband ignored three citations without consequence.

The experience of Rodi Alvorada Peña shows some of the many ways in which states around the world fail to fulfil their responsibilities for the protection of women. Acts of violence against women must be prohibited in law as criminal offences. However, this alone is not sufficient to ensure freedom from torture or ill-treatment.

The UN Declaration on the Elimination of Violence against Women (see Box, page 25) and the Fourth UN World Conference on Women held in Beijing in 1995 set out steps for governments to take to eliminate violence against women.[29] These include reviewing national legislation to ensure its effectiveness in eliminating violence against women and emphasizing the prosecution of offenders, providing women with access to the mechanisms of justice for effective remedies, and promoting policies to reduce violence against women, including with law enforcement officers, police personnel and judicial, medical and social workers. The implementation of such steps is one indicator for measuring a state's willingness and ability to protect women against acts of torture.

As the UN Special Rapporteur on violence against

An AI member at the Pride celebration in Paris, France, holds a poster drawing attention to human rights abuses against lesbians and gays. State and community regulation of women's sexuality often renders women vulnerable to violence and degrading treatment.

23

women has noted, "the due diligence standard is not limited to legislation or criminalization"[30] but encompasses a whole range of approaches including training of state personnel, education, "demystifying domestic violence" and other measures.[31]

Apologists for violence against women, including governments, have sometimes argued that customs and traditions which result in abuse of women must be respected as genuine manifestations of a nation's or community's culture and may not be subjected to scrutiny from the perspective of human rights. Such views fail to recognize that cultural practices are sometimes both the context of human rights violations and a justification for them, concealing an unwillingness to take positive action to end discriminatory practices.

AI welcomes the rich diversity of cultures and believes that the universality of human rights, far from denying diversity, can only benefit from it. The contribution of different cultures enriches the understanding of human rights, giving them their local form and language. While recognizing the importance of cultural diversity, AI stands resolutely in defence of the universality of all human rights, including the

Beirut, Lebanon, September 2000. Thousands of women in Lebanon took part in a march for women's rights, and against sexual discrimination and violence, as part of the World March of Women.

fundamental rights to life and to freedom from torture and ill-treatment. The duty of the state is to ensure the full protection of these rights, where necessary moderating tradition through education and the law. As the Special Rapporteur on violence against women has pointed out, "States have an affirmative obligation to confront those cultural practices of the community which result in violence against women and which degrade and humiliate women, thereby denying women the full enjoyment of their human rights. International standards require that there be concerted State policy to eradicate these practices even if their proponents argue that they have their roots in religious beliefs and rituals."[32]

> **UN Declaration on the Elimination of Violence against Women, Extract from Article 4:**
>
> States should condemn violence against women and should not invoke any custom, tradition or religious consideration to avoid their obligations with respect to its elimination. States should pursue by all appropriate means and without delay a policy of eliminating violence against women and, to this end, should:
>
> (a) Consider, where they have not yet done so, ratifying or acceding to the Convention on the Elimination of All Forms of Discrimination against Women or withdrawing reservations to that Convention;
>
> (b) Refrain from engaging in violence against women;
>
> (c) Exercise due diligence to prevent, investigate and, in accordance with national legislation, punish acts of violence against women, whether those acts are perpetrated by the State or by private persons;
>
> (d) Develop penal, civil, labour and administrative sanctions in domestic legislation to punish and redress the wrongs caused to women who are subjected to violence; women who are subjected to violence should be provided with access to the mechanisms of justice and, as provided for by national legislation, to just and effective remedies for the harm that they have suffered; States should also inform women of their rights in seeking redress through such mechanisms;
>
> (e) Consider the possibility of developing national plans of action to promote the protection of women against any form of violence, or to include provisions for that purpose in plans already existing, taking into account, as appropriate, such cooperation as can be provided by non-governmental organizations, particularly those concerned with the issue of violence against women;

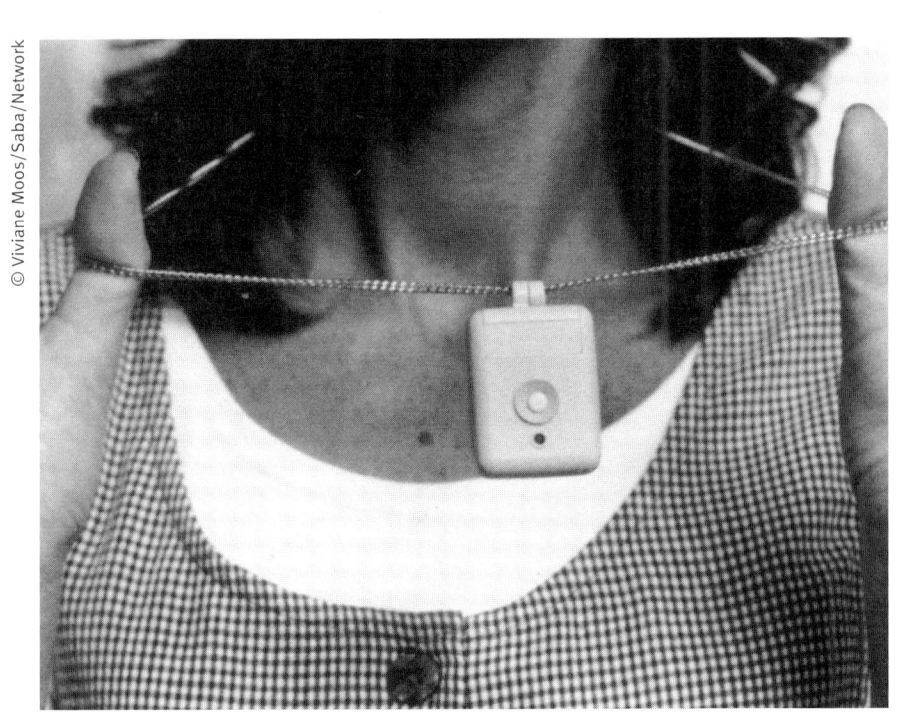

Failure to provide legal redress

Governments around the world have failed to fulfil their duty to secure legal redress for abused women. Gender discrimination in this area includes the persistence of inadequate laws against abuses and institutional failings on the part of the criminal justice process, including the police and the judiciary. Often these failings mutually reinforce each other.

Many abuses against women are not treated as criminal offences in national law. Laws governing rape are inadequate in many countries. Most countries do not have a law against marital rape: the preliminary results of a survey undertaken by the women's non-governmental organization Change indicate that worldwide, only 27 countries have legislated against rape in marriage.[33] Forced marriage is not recognized as an offence in many countries and trafficking is more often criminalized in terms of law and order or illegal migration than with a view to protecting the rights of the victims.

A woman wears a crisis alarm that should bring prompt help if she is attacked. As part of a domestic violence project, in Schenectady, New York, USA, courts give women these alarms in cases where they believe the women are in serious danger from their husbands.

> The failure of a government to prohibit acts of violence against women, or to establish adequate legal protection against such acts, constitutes a failure of state protection. Acts of violence against women constitute torture when they are of the nature and severity envisaged by the concept of torture and the state has failed to provide effective protection.

Lack of redress for trafficked women

Trafficked women find it particularly difficult to obtain redress as in many parts of the world they are treated as criminals rather than as victims.[34] Trafficking involves the recruitment, transportation, purchase or sale of human beings by violence, abduction, force, fraud, deception, coercion or debt bondage, for the purpose of exploitation.[35]

In December 1998, 53 trafficked Asian women were arrested in Toronto along with agents and pimps who had brought the women to the country illegally and had forced them into prostitution to repay the debt for their transport to Canada. The women were charged with prostitution related offences and offences under the Immigration Act. The traffickers were not charged with torture or sexual slavery but with the lesser charge of forcible confinement. "Law enforcement agents were hesitant to label the operation sexual slavery owing to the existence of 'contracts', under which the women's travel documents were confiscated, their movements restricted and they were forced to work off their debt by performing 400-500 sex acts. Because the women had agreed to migrate to work in the sex trade, law enforcement agents concluded that 'they knew exactly what they were getting into'."[36]

The Human Rights Committee, commenting on the treatment of trafficked women in Israel, stated that it "regrets that women brought to Israel for the purpose of prostitution, many of whom are brought as a result of false pretences or coercion, are not protected as victims of trafficking but are likely to bear the penalties of their illegal presence in Israel by deportation. Such an approach to this problem effectively prevents these women from pursuing a remedy for the violation of their rights under article 8 of the Covenant [which prohibits slavery]. The Committee recommends that serious efforts be made to seek out and punish the traffickers, to institute rehabilitation programmes for the victims and to ensure that they are able to pursue legal remedies against the perpetrators."37 In July 2000 the Israeli parliament made the buying and selling of human beings for the purposes of prostitution a criminal offence.

The Special Rapporteur on violence against women has pointed out that: *"Anti-immigration policies aid and abet traffickers. ...inflexible policies of exclusion, which are enforced through severe punishments of a penal nature and deportation for its breach, feed directly into the hands of traffickers... Trafficking economies — which arise out of a combination of supply, demand and illegality — are less likely to develop in situations in which opportunities exist for legal migrant work."*38

© Kayte Brimacombe/Network

Lack of redress for women who have been raped

In India, the law with regard to evidence in rape case allows that "When a man is prosecuted for rape or an attempt to ravish, it may be shown that the prosecutrix was of generally immoral character."39 On the other hand, the character of the accused may not be taken into account.40 This provision makes it almost impossible for women who work as prostitutes to obtain redress for rape. In addition, Indian law

Women in Pakistan who have been raped, but cannot provide four witnesses to prove that they did not give consent, have themselves been jailed for illicit sexual intercourse. Lock-up, Karachi Central Court, Pakistan.

does not require police to send women who allege rape for an immediate medical examination, so that frequently medical evidence is lost.

There are specific legal hurdles in Pakistan to reporting sexual abuse. The law relating to rape is such that if women victims of rape fail to establish lack of consent, they may themselves become accused of *zina* (fornication). *Zina* is an offence punishable by stoning to death or public flogging. Women's groups have campaigned for changes in the law to enable rape victims to report the crime without risk to themselves, but without success. In these circumstances, AI considers that the government is complicit in the torture of women.

Restrictions which hamper redress

Restrictions on women's freedom of movement, initiatives and legal rights may further hamper access to justice for women victims of violence.

Women in Saudi Arabia who leave their home to seek help from the police run the risk of arrest for being in public unaccompanied by a male relative such as a brother or uncle, and are usually taken back to the abusive situation they seek to flee. In Pakistan, women in rural areas rarely know their way about in the world outside their immediate family land, have no access to money, and would arouse instant suspicion if they walked outside their village or took a bus.

In some countries, women cannot go to court in person — their male relatives are supposed to represent their interests. For example, in Saudi Arabia it is considered shameful for a woman to appear in court to assert her rights.

Inappropriate legal responses

In some cases, governments have passed legislation against abuses which has in fact led to further human rights violations. Responding to a 10 per cent increase in reports of rape over the previous year, the government of Swaziland in May 2000 was reportedly finalizing legislation to chemically castrate convicted rapists. The proposed law not only risks violating the prohibition of cruel, inhuman and degrading punishment, it also treats rape as solely about sexual gratification. But rape is essentially "about a way to exert power over another. Impotent men have committed rape with beer bottles."[41]

Similarly, the Pakistan government in March 1997 extended the death penalty to gang rape; it had previously been punishable by 25 years' imprisonment. The Indian government has also introduced legislation which would punish rape with the death penalty, as a "populist" response to the crime. AI considers that the death penalty is itself a breach of human rights. In none of the countries which have introduced the death penalty for gang rape has the incidence of such crimes declined. In the Philippines, out of more than 1,500 people on death row, at least half were convicted of rape, yet reports of rape have continued to rise. AI is resolutely opposed to punishments which themselves violate human rights, such as judicial corporal punishment and the death penalty.

Failure to investigate: gender bias in the police

International standards require that complaints and reports of violence against women be promptly, impartially and effectively investigated. However, the reality is often sadly different. In many parts of the world, the police routinely fail to investigate abuses reported by women, treating violence in the home not as a criminal matter or a human rights concern, but as a domestic affair for which they have no responsibility. For women belonging to racial, ethnic or religious minorities, the police are often even more reluctant to intervene, either on spurious grounds of "cultural sensitivity" or through racial prejudice.

Gender bias among police is rarely addressed by governments, despite their international obligation to eradicate it. Rarely do the authorities investigate allegations of bias, apply appropriate disciplinary measures to police officers who

> The failure of a state to investigate allegations of violence against women constitutes a failure of state protection. Acts of violence against women constitute torture when they are of the nature and severity envisaged by the concept of torture and the state has failed to provide effective protection.

discriminate against women victims and train all police officers in how to deal with allegations of violence against women. Few recruit sufficient women police officers, essential because in many societies women victims of violence find it difficult to tell male police officers intimate details about the physical abuses they have suffered.

Police often share the attitudes of perpetrators of violence against women and consciously or unconsciously shield the offenders. They frequently send abused women back home rather than file complaints. Sometimes they advise mediation and reconciliation without realizing that the women who approach them have usually compromised and accepted as much as they could bear. In many instances, police have humiliated victims, adding to their suffering rather than alleviating it.

A study on domestic violence in Thailand said that battered women were stigmatized in society and ignored by the criminal justice system, making legal redress rare. Police habitually advised women to reconcile with their partners after violence. If women insisted on prosecution they generally had to bribe police to pursue the case. The study found that the police and judiciary did not consider cases of rape and domestic abuse important.[42]

In India, when women victims of domestic violence approach the police, they are often pressured to compromise with the offender. Even when victims insist, police are reluctant to file criminal complaints. Rape victims seeking to file complaints are often ridiculed.

Abused women are reluctant to seek police help for a variety of reasons. According to the UK's British Crime Survey, most women only report domestic violence after repeated assaults and most abused women conceal their injuries for fear of further infuriating the abuser, out of shame or because they believe themselves somehow at fault. Canadian government statistics indicate that more than 75 per cent of women seriously

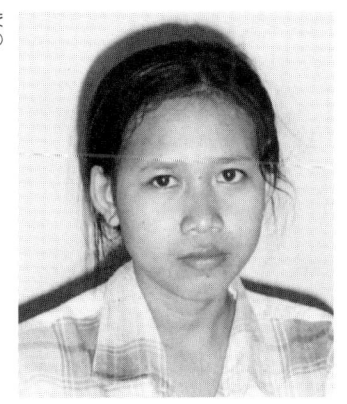

Saudi Arabia: Karsini Binti Sandi, an Indonesian domestic worker, was abused by her employers and threatened by the police when she sought their help. She escaped to Indonesia in January 2000.

assaulted by their husbands did not report the incident to police.

Sometimes women do not attempt to seek police help as they know this to be futile. A Saudi Arabian woman explained: "My husband was very violent. There were about five occasions when he beat me so badly that I needed hospital treatment... There was no point my going to the police ... it is well known in Saudi Arabia that the police would not have helped; they would have simply sent me back to my husband. In any event, my husband has a very senior position and the police are unlikely to have wanted to intervene."[43]

Women who tell police in the UK that they fear abduction and forced marriage frequently face inaction. Often this "appears to be due to ingrained gender and cultural biases, specifically the assumption that forced marriage is a 'family matter' and a practice rooted in religious beliefs or cultural practices, and therefore does not require external intervention".[44] In one case, a young woman who was returned to her family by UK police despite expressing her fear of abduction was taken to India and forced into marriage. She was eventually traced and returned to the UK.[45]

Failure to prosecute and punish: gender bias of courts

Bhanwari Devi, a village development worker active in trying to eradicate child marriage in India, was raped on 22 September 1992 in Bhateri village, Rajasthan, by five men of a higher caste. Police initially refused to record Bhanwari Devi's statement, and she was also refused a medical examination. An inquiry, set up by the government after much protest, reportedly subjected her to a gruelling and intrusive interrogation. The inquiry found her allegations true and a charge sheet was filed against five men. The trial began in a lower court in November 1994. In a verdict given in November 1995, the court found that the delay in filing her complaint with police and in obtaining a medical examination indicated that she had made the story up. The court observed that the incident could not have taken place because upper caste men

Switzerland: a demonstration for women's rights in October 2000 — part of the World March of Women.

would not rape a woman of a lower caste. The men were acquitted of the charge of gang rape but convicted of minor crimes. Throughout, she was pressured to withdraw the case by members of the local community and politicians.

Judges are part of the society in which they live, reflecting its cultural values, moral norms and its prejudices. Rising above prejudice is a prerequisite of judicial office, but discrimination against women and lack of understanding of violence against women as a human rights issue frequently lead to bias in the way trials are conducted and in decisions and rulings.

In Italy, in February 1999, the Supreme Court (Court of Cassation) overturned an appeal court verdict which had found a male driving instructor guilty of raping his 18-year-old student. The Supreme Court, noting that the victim was wearing jeans at the time of the offence, commented: "It is common knowledge...that jeans cannot even be partly removed without the active cooperation of the person wearing them....and it is impossible if the victim is struggling with all her force". The court decided that this indicated that she had consented to sex and concluded that the rape was not proven, referring the case back to another appeal court for retrial.

In June 1997, the Mexican Supreme Court decided that marital rape was not rape, only the "undue exercise of a right". The decision was later nullified by Congress.

The National Commission for Women in India said in its Annual Report for 1995-96 regarding the obstacles women face in rape cases: "Not many of these cases reach the courts for trial, partly in view of the shame and honour involved and partly due to the existing difficult and complicated procedural laws. It was also noticed that the police are generally apathetic to the registration of complaints involving rape. Even in those cases which come to courts for trial ... our courts had not been sensitive to the trauma undergone by the rape victims, both during the actual commission of the offence and during trial in the courts. The courts are also oblivious to the social stigma and ostracism a victim of rape has to face throughout her life ..."

Women in the Philippines rarely report rape and sexual harassment to the authorities. It is extremely difficult for a woman to report a rape to the police and follow it through to trial. Media reporting is generally sensationalist and intrusive, and cases take years to go through the courts. Judges are reported to have dismissed cases, including against police officers, partly based on their belief that the woman was sexually experienced.

Gender bias among those responsible for administering justice is further aggravated by problems within the legal framework relating to issues such as the codification of rape and sexual offences, the definition of consent, the nature of the evidence required and the rules governing cross-examination of victims. Such factors often further alienate and dehumanize women victims, and lead to very low conviction rates for crimes of violence against women throughout the world. In addition, worldwide there are too few women judges to hear cases of abuse.

Laws in many parts of the world permit the past sexual history of women victims of rape to be discussed in court, humiliating and distressing them, and allowing the defence to portray the victim as "loose". Until changes were introduced into UK law in July 2000, men accused of rape or sexual assault who represented themselves in court could cross-examine victims with little or no restraint, forcing them to relive in public every detail of their ordeal.

In Nigeria, women who have been raped may be unable to obtain justice and deterred from reporting offences for fear of being punished themselves. Punishments include public floggings. Bariya Ibrahim Magazu, aged 17, was sentenced to 180 strokes of the cane in Zamfara State in northern Nigeria in early September 2000. She had no legal representation and was unable to produce witnesses to substantiate her claim that three men had forced themselves on her and that one had made her pregnant. She was sentenced to 100 lashes for having sexual relations outside marriage and a further 80 lashes for her accusations against the three men, which were judged to be false. The sentence was carried out in January 2001, after the delivery of the baby.

In late September 2000, also in Zamfara State, Aishat Dutsi and her husband Haruna were given 80 lashes each in public for making an allegedly false accusation that a village leader had had sexual relations with their daughter. The Nigerian Federal Government has advised citizens whose constitutional rights have been violated in state courts to seek legal redress in the higher courts, including the Supreme Court. However, sentences are often carried out immediately after conviction and most defendants have no means to bring an appeal. It is unclear what action the Federal Government has taken to protect such individuals from harsh corporal punishment; it is not known to have sought injunctions in the courts, for example, to prevent punishments being carried out.

In many countries, women seeking justice face insuperable economic obstacles. Lack of money, as well as educational deprivation, militate against women seeking and obtaining legal redress for abuses they suffer. Rights awareness programs and legal aid are sorely lacking where they are needed most. In some countries corruption permeates the judiciary, and more men than women are in a position to offer financial inducements to obtain the outcome they want.

While judges often take a lenient view of men abusing women, many have failed to consider severe domestic violence suffered by women as relevant when assessing women's responsibility for offences committed by them. Indravani Pamela Ramjattan was sentenced to death in May 1995 in Trinidad and Tobago for the murder of her common law husband in 1991. During her trial lawyers introduced evidence of the years of abuse and violence she had suffered — including beatings, death threats and rape. Despite this evidence she was convicted of murder, which has a mandatory death sentence. In 1999, an appeal court reduced her murder conviction to manslaughter and sentenced her to a total of 13 years' imprisonment, based on psychiatric evidence which showed that at the time of the murder she was suffering from "Battered Women's Syndrome".

In November 1999, a Sri Lankan domestic worker was sentenced to two months' imprisonment in Dubai after she tore up a copy of the Koran to protest against six months of sexual abuse by her employer and his two sons. She reported the abuse in court and said she had found no way to escape. Court officials responded by advising families with non-Muslim maids to keep the holy texts out of their reach. There was no report of any inquiry into her allegation of rape, let alone any prosecution.

> The failure of a state to prosecute and punish those responsible for violence against women constitutes a failure of state protection. Acts of violence against women constitute torture when they are of the nature and severity envisaged by the concept of torture and the state has failed to provide effective protection.

Social and cultural hurdles to redress

Women may not be able to obtain redress for abuses for a variety of reasons. Many arise because women are deprived of their economic, social and cultural rights.

Economic dependence and inadequate welfare provision in many parts of the world force women to bear continued abuse. Abused women often have nowhere to go, no money to sustain themselves or their children, and no funds to seek legal counsel in order to pursue redress. Legal aid is often not available to abused women. Social and economic deprivation go hand in hand with ignorance of legal rights and the criminal justice process, so women are often unaware of their alternatives. They may justifiably fear further humiliation by police and the risk of being sent back to further abuse. They may also fear for their safety or their children's safety, or that they will lose custody of their children. According to the British Crime Survey, for example, most women only reported domestic violence after having suffered violent abuse some 35 to 40 times.

Non-governmental organizations throughout the world have taken on many of the state's duties in the areas of support and redress for women victims of abuse, providing shelter, emotional support, legal aid and temporary financial assistance. They suffer, however, from lack of resources. In France, for example, the government helps to fund just two telephone hotlines for the entire country, one of which is directed towards victims of domestic violence and the other to victims of rape.[46]

Shelters for abused women, whether state-run or operated by non-governmental organizations, are almost everywhere inadequately funded or too few in numbers to provide assistance to the women in need. In Saudi Arabia, women's associations are controlled by the government and women's refuges do not exist. Pakistan's state-run refuges are only accessible to women by order of a magistrate, and hold women in quasi-detention.

In some countries the lack of women's shelters has led to women being imprisoned for their own protection while their abusers remain free. In Jordan, many women prisoners stay in jail after they have served their sentence as they do not feel safe returning to their families. The Director of the Women's Correctional and Rehabilitation Centre said in July 2000 that 35 out of 214 women were currently behind bars in "protective custody for fear of what their families might do to them... Some women are spending indefinite periods in prison, some are not convicted of any offence and others have served their sentence but can't be released because we fear for their safety".[47]

Domestic violence does not only damage the body. It can also undermine or destroy a woman's self-esteem and her will to resist abuse and seek redress. The subordination of women to men is still widely accepted in all cultures, even by women, and presumed to be authorized by "natural order", religion or tradition. A study of sexual violence in the heavily populated southern metropolitan districts of Johannesburg, South Africa,[48] revealed that girls and women, especially those living in poverty, tolerated sexual violence and

Anastazia Baláñova's sister-in-law holds her bloodstained nightdress. On 20 August 2000, three men broke into a Romani home in Zilina, northern Slovakia, and beat Anastazia Baláñova and her daughters with baseball bats. Anastazia died three days later and two of the children were injured. Although the authorities reacted promptly in this case, the failure of the state to protect victims of anti-Romani violence and to prosecute those responsible has contributed to an atmosphere in which racist violence against Roma by skinhead gangs has spread.

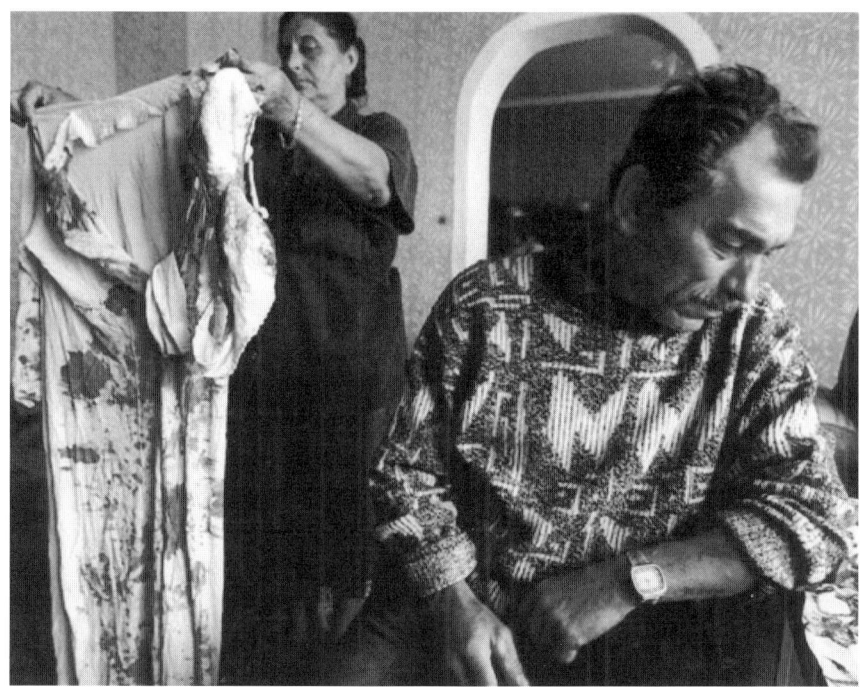

© Julie Denesha/The Prague Post

discrimination to a surprising degree. More than half the women interviewed believed that women were partly responsible for sexual abuse, and 12 per cent of young women did not believe they had a right to resist abuse.

Abuses are often borne silently by women as their accepted fate — indeed women frequently feel responsible for the harm done to them. In many cultures women are socially defined only in relation to their fathers or husbands. To leave the family home because of abuse requires extraordinary courage and may result in social isolation and harassment over and above the abuse suffered. Women must bear the stigma of divorce or a failed relationship, of disrupting the family.

Traditionally, married women are presumed to have given permanent consent to sex with their husbands and to have no right to refuse. Similarly, women employed in the sex industry are often assumed to have foregone their right to refuse intercourse and their resistance to enforced sex is considered unjustified. Nepali women who had been trafficked into Indian brothels, rescued by non-governmental organizations and taken home, were ostracized by their communities, as they were seen as immoral rather than as victims of a cruel trade.[49]

The failure of the state to ensure women's enjoyment of social, economic and cultural rights further hinders their access to redress for acts of violence and facilitates continuing torture and ill-treatment.

Victoriana Vázquez Sánchez (left), a 50-year-old member of the Mixteca indigenous community of Barrio Nuevo San José, Guerrero state, Mexico, was reportedly raped by Mexican soldiers in April 1999. With another woman relative, she had left the community to look for a young man and a boy from their family who had gone to harvest crops and had not returned. The two women were allegedly captured and raped by soldiers near their plots of land. The bodies of their two relatives were found more than two weeks later.

3: Torture by state agents and armed groups

Women have been tortured by police, soldiers and other officials in countries all over the world. Women of all ages, ethnic groups, classes and creeds have been subjected to physical and sexual violence in custody or at the hands of armed political groups.

Torture is used as an instrument of political repression, isolating and punishing women who challenge the prevailing order, whether non-violently or by taking up arms. However, the majority of women victims of torture by state agents are people suspected of criminal offences.

In many countries, severe beatings and other physical and psychological abuse are standard practice for arrested criminal suspects or marginalized women who come into contact with the law. In the majority of countries, the racial, ethnic or religious background of the women, or their poverty, render them especially vulnerable to acts of torture or ill-treatment.

Costa Rica, outside the Supreme Court, November 1999: women dressed in black call for an end to violence against women.

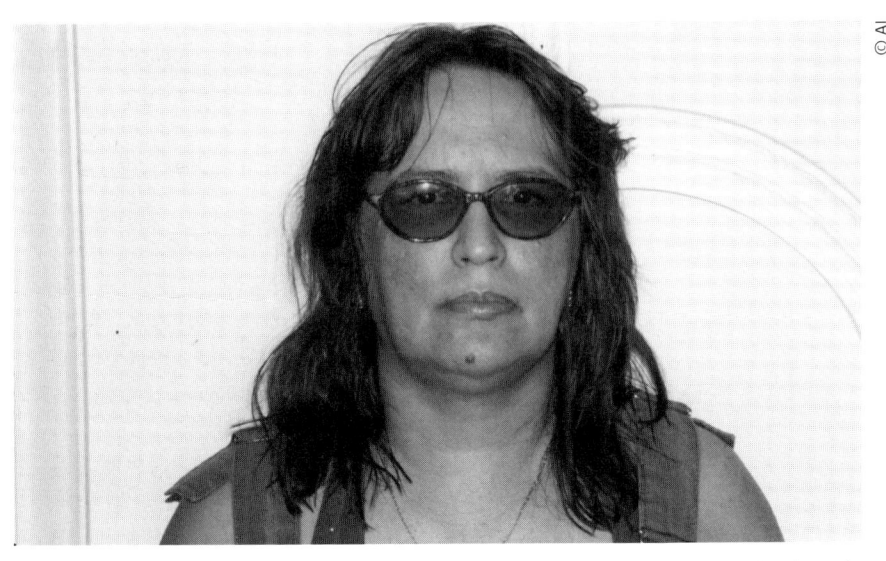

Torture of women in custody

AI has investigated countless incidents of torture or cruel treatment of women in custody by police officers, prison guards, soldiers and other officials. Women in custody have been subjected to all the terrible methods of inflicting pain that torturers have devised. They have been beaten, subjected to electric shocks, mock executions and death threats, sleep deprivation and sensory deprivation. They have been suspended by the hands or feet, beaten on the soles of the feet, suffocated and submerged in water.

In many countries, acts of sexual violence by government agents are a common method of torture or inhuman treatment inflicted on women.[50] Such acts include rape and other forms of sexual abuse, "virginity testing", sexually offensive language and touching.

Torture and ill-treatment of women in custody is a daily reality. From January to September 2000 alone, AI documented cases in countries including Bangladesh, China, Democratic Republic of Congo, Ecuador, Egypt, France, India, Israel, Kenya,

Lucia Paiva de Almeida has been unable to leave her home in the suburbs of Rio de Janeiro, Brazil, for four years. Lucia and her husband were arrested without warrant in 1996 by members of the civil police. Lucia was physically and sexually tortured in a small room in the police station as police tried to force her to implicate her husband in a number of thefts. She was then put out onto the street in the early hours of the morning. No one has been charged in connection with her torture. Lucia has panic attacks and palpitations, and is presently receiving treatment from an AI-funded project. She says that if she recovers enough, her first outing will be to go shopping with her son.

Lebanon, Nepal, Pakistan, Philippines, Russia, Saudi Arabia, Spain, Sri Lanka, Sudan, Tajikistan, Turkey and the USA.

In the USA, torture and ill-treatment of incarcerated women includes beatings; rape and other forms of sexual abuse; the cruel, inhuman or degrading use of restraints on women prisoners, including those who are pregnant or seriously ill; inadequate access to medical treatment; terrible conditions in isolation units, and harsh and punitive labour. Allegations of sexual abuse of women prisoners in the USA nearly always involve male staff who, contrary to international standards, are allowed unsupervised access to female jail and prison inmates in many jurisdictions.

In China, many women, particularly migrant workers, have been detained, accused of prostitution, and subjected to rape and sexual abuse. Police have the power to issue an instant fine on suspicion of prostitution and may hold alleged prostitutes and their clients in administrative detention for up to two years. There are frequent reports of police detaining and ill-treating women to extract lists of "clients" for blackmail. Such practices have become so common that in recent years they have been revealed as a major source of income for many police stations in different areas. Many alleged prostitutes and clients have died in custody as a result of torture or ill-treatment. Others have committed suicide shortly after release, believing their lives had been ruined by the stigma of these allegations and the degradation of the abuse they have suffered.

Women in police custody in the Philippines are vulnerable to torture or ill-treatment, including rape, sexual abuse, threats, slaps, punches and kicks. The most marginalized members of society are particularly at risk, especially prostitutes, street children (many of whom leave home to escape abuse in the family), drug users and the impoverished. In many cases, police use the anti-vagrancy law — legislation which discriminates against the poor and women in particular — to extort money and sexually abuse women. Sexual harassment and abuse, including rape, also occurs in jails.

In Turkey, torture of women prisoners is a widespread practice. Torture methods repeatedly reported to AI include electro-shocks and beatings directed at the breasts and genitals, being stripped naked, and sexual abuse including rape and threats of rape.

Women are tortured not only in police stations, prisons, military barracks and other official buildings belonging to security agencies. They are also tortured by state agents in unofficial or secret detention centres, in the victim's home, or on the street. For example, in the Democratic Republic of the Congo, women detained in Kinshasa are routinely the object of torture, particularly rape. In 1999 Jeannine Bouchez Mwayuma was taken by a military officer and several soldiers to a hotel in the Kintambo district of Kinshasa, where they interrogated and raped her.

Many countries use methods of punishment against women detainees which constitute torture or cruel, inhuman or degrading treatment. In Saudi Arabia, for instance, "moral crimes", which women are more likely to be accused of than men,[51] may be punished by flogging. In one US state, women prisoners have been punished by being held for hours in an eight by four feet (2.4 by 1.2 metres) cage or "detention trailer" — in temperatures of more than 100 degrees Fahrenheit (38 degrees Centigrade). According to a former prisoner, the prisoners were made to stand in the cage and denied bathroom facilities, causing them sometimes to defecate or urinate while in the cage. They were hosed off and "watered" every 90 minutes. According to the testimony, prisoners on hard labour assignments were made to do gratuitously harsh and punitive labour and often punished with the cage because they could not keep up with the work.[52] Texas officials denied the treatment was inhumane but confirmed that "any offender refusing to perform her assigned duties will be secured in the detention trailer for the duration of the work period".

Women who have suffered violence in custody face a long and arduous struggle for justice. Female prisoners generally find

The fathers of two young women tortured by police in Turkey in March 1999 hold AI's appeal on behalf of their daughters. Fatma Deniz Polattas, aged 19, and 16-year-old N.C.S. were held naked and blindfolded, beaten and sexually abused, and Fatma Deniz Polattas was raped.

it extraordinarily difficult to stop unlawful conduct or to have a perpetrator brought to justice. The victim may have good reason to fear that if she complains she will be victimized again, or that investigators will not believe her word in the face of denial by a guard.

Many reports of abuses are not even investigated. The failure of officials to investigate allegations of torture not only allows torturers to go unpunished, but often contributes to unfair trials and unjust imprisonment when statements extracted under torture are used as evidence.

If investigations do take place, complaints of torture or ill-treatment of women in custody rarely result in law enforcement officers being disciplined or convicted, even in cases where there seems to be overwhelming evidence that an offence has been committed. The lack of political will to prosecute law enforcement officers suspected of raping or sexually abusing women in their custody creates a climate of impunity, contributing to further human rights abuses against women.

Sexual violence against women in custody

- Rape of women detainees by prison, security or military officials always amounts to torture. Other forms of sexual violence committed by law enforcement officials may constitute either torture or cruel, inhuman or degrading treatment.

- Sexual violence against a woman detainee by a security, military or police official cannot be deemed a "personal" or private act. A number of decisions by international and regional bodies have supported the argument that rape by such officials always amounts to torture[53], even if committed in the victim's home.[54]

- According to international standards[55], sexual violence by inmates against other inmates may also constitute torture or ill-treatment. The prison authorities are responsible for protecting inmates, and if they fail to ensure compliance with rules such as the separation of women and men, this can be tantamount to acquiescence in sexual violence.

- Practices such as allowing male staff to search women prisoners, and allowing male staff to patrol areas where women may be viewed in their cells while dressing, washing or taking showers, constitute inhuman and degrading treatment.

Broken bodies, shattered minds

Photo credit: ©Jenny Matthews/Network

Sierra Leone. This 38-year-old woman had her arm cut off by rebel forces who attacked her farm in 1997. She is now at the Murray Town camp for amputees in Freetown, where she has been fitted with an artificial arm and is relearning skills such as planting.

Torture of women in armed conflict

In all the armed conflicts investigated by AI in 1999 and 2000, torture of women, including rape, was reported. Torture by soldiers of vanquished women has a long history — a history of subjugation, terror and revenge. Armed conflicts are not only about men in battlefields, nor are they gender-neutral exercises in destruction. Evidence gathered by human rights organizations and by international and national tribunals indicates that women are targeted because of their gender, and that the forms of abuses inflicted upon them tend to be gender-specific.

Women are frequently singled out for torture in armed conflicts because of their role as educators and as symbols of the community. Tutsi women in the 1994 genocide in Rwanda, and Muslim, Serb, Croat and ethnic Albanian women in the former Yugoslavia, were tortured because they were women of a particular ethnic, national or religious group.

Most abuses committed against women in armed conflicts involve the use of sexual violence. Sexual violence is often a gruesome, ritualized prologue to murder. In the east of the Democratic Republic of the Congo, many women killed in the most recent bout of conflict (1999-2000) are reported to have been found completely naked and bearing signs of having been raped.

In Guatemala, during the civil war of the 1970s and 1980s, massacres of Mayan villagers were preceded by the rape of women and girls. In December 1982, for example, Guatemalan soldiers entered the village of Dos Erres, La Libertad, in the northern department of Petén. By the time they left three days later, it is estimated that more than 350 people — men, women and children — had been

Bosnian Muslim women in the Tuzla refugee camp (northeast Bosnia). These women were systematically raped by Serb militiamen during the war which ripped the former Yugoslavia apart between 1991 and 1995. They agreed to be photographed in order to ensure that "the world knows the truth" about the war in Bosnia.

©Rex Features Ltd/Andrée Kaiser - Sipa Press

killed. The women and girls had been subjected to mass rape before being slaughtered. The investigation into this massacre has been hampered by repeated death threats and acts of intimidation against relatives of the victims and members of forensic teams. Eighteen years later, no one has been brought to justice, despite detailed eye-witness accounts.

In Algeria, hundreds of women have been abducted and tortured since 1993 by armed groups which define themselves as "Islamic groups". Especially in rural areas, women have been

Argentinian women, representing the Mothers of the Plaza de Mayo, demonstrate outside the Naval Mechanics School (ESMA), in Buenos Aires, notorious for having been used as a torture centre in Argentina in the 1970s and early 1980s. The women are protesting against a plan to destroy the building and replace it with a monument to national unity.

abducted from their homes by armed groups, held captive, raped and subjected to other forms of torture — such as beatings, burning with cigarettes and death threats. Many were subsequently killed and some left permanently disabled. Some victims were raped by more than one member of the armed group.

Rape and other forms of sexual violence against girls and women by rebel forces have been systematic and widespread during the nine-year internal armed conflict in Sierra Leone. Mutilations (especially deliberate amputations) committed during the conflict have received considerable international attention, but sexual violence has been even more prevalent. Almost all the thousands of girls and women who have been abducted by rebel forces have been raped and forced into sexual slavery. Sexual violence has been directed at women of all ages, including very young girls. An 11-year-old girl abducted from Freetown when rebel forces attacked the capital in January 1999 was freed seven months later. She described being dragged from her home and then joined by scores of other girls as rebel forces went from house to house. Girls who were not selected to be the "wife" of a rebel commander were repeatedly raped by countless other rebel combatants.

Almost all rape victims in Sierra Leone have required medical treatment for physical injuries inflicted during their ordeal. A 29-year-old woman who fled the town of Makeni in Northern Province in May 2000 told AI representatives a month later: " I'm still breast-feeding but five RUF rebels raped me. I'm still bleeding". Most rape victims have contracted sexually transmitted diseases, and many are suspected of having contracted HIV/AIDS. No one knows how many pregnancies and childbirths have resulted.[56]

Acts of torture in armed conflict are committed within a context characterized by the breakdown of the policing or judicial system. The normal restraints on acts of violence against women are therefore missing. Hardship and deprivation also force women to "submit" to non-consensual sexual relations. Armed conflicts and ensuing displacement lead to an increase in all forms of violence, including domestic violence against women.[57]

> **'Disappearances'**
> In war-torn regions many women have lost relatives, either because they have been separated and lost, because they have been killed, or because they have "disappeared" — taken into secret custody, with the authorities concealing their fate and whereabouts. Women are unable to discover what has happened to their family members, where they might be, or even if they are alive or dead. The search for the truth may last for years; in some cases it never ends. Many women face severe financial hardships if the main breadwinner "disappears". They often cannot dispose of property to sustain the family, and cannot remarry, because their status is unclear.
>
> Under international human rights law, relatives and dependants of a "disappeared" person are also considered to be victims of the crime of "disappearance". In the majority of the cases, those relatives and dependants are mothers, wives, or daughters. International human rights bodies and tribunals have held that the psychological anguish and distress caused to the relatives of people who have "disappeared" is itself a violation of the prohibition against torture and other cruel, inhuman or degrading treatment or punishment.[58]

Violence against women is not an accident of war: it is a weapon of war used for such purposes as spreading terror; destabilizing a society and breaking its resistance; rewarding soldiers; and extracting information. Violence against women, including torture, has also been used as a method of "ethnic cleansing" and as an element of genocide. In most of the situations investigated by AI, there is evidence that the military has used violence against women for several of these purposes.

Women who have been tortured in conflicts are often unable to gain access to medical and legal remedies. Investigations conducted in areas including the former Yugoslavia, northern Uganda, eastern Congo and India have demonstrated that most victims fail to admit they have been raped for fear of being stigmatized by society or rejected by their husbands. Evidence also shows that this fear is well-founded: women who have been raped have been unable to find marriage partners, and those who were married are often deserted by their husbands.

Torture of women escaping conflict

For many women and girls, there is no safe way to escape from war zones. Women who leave in boats are frequently attacked by pirates. Women who travel by road are assaulted by bandits, security forces, border guards, smugglers and other refugees. Refugees are often forced to turn to smugglers as the only way to cross the border and escape. Women in this situation are frequently abused by smugglers who offer to help them in exchange for sex.

Internally displaced and refugee women living in camps may face sexual and physical abuse. Camp guards and male refugees may look upon unaccompanied women and girls as common sexual property. Women who have already been raped may be treated as having lost their virtue and may therefore be preyed upon. They also have to bear the physical and psychological damage of the trauma they have suffered without adequate medical support or counselling.[59] Often, domestic violence against women escalates in refugee camps. In many camps the physical conditions increase the likelihood of violence against women: camps may be overcrowded and their design and location can render women particularly vulnerable to attacks both from within and outside the camp. Discrimination against women in the

Women and children reaching safety at a reception centre in Eritrea for internally displaced people fleeing renewed fighting in May 2000 in the Ethiopia/Eritrea border. Most of the world's refugees and internally displaced people are women and children.

distribution of goods and services may lead to sexual abuse of refugee women rendered vulnerable by hardship.

Women who reach other countries and apply for asylum face continuing difficulties in their search for safety. Many governments, eager to avoid their responsibility to provide protection for refugees, are applying an increasingly restrictive definition of who qualifies for refugee status. A number of countries deny refugee status to people persecuted by armed opposition groups, and few countries grant asylum where the state has failed to protect against torture by private individuals.

Women asylum-seekers
- The definition of a refugee in international refugee law (the 1951 Convention relating to the Status of Refugees and its 1967 Protocol) remains applicable in situations where an entire group has been displaced and members of the group are at risk of human rights violations because of some shared characteristic.
- International protection is due to those whom the state is unwilling or unable to protect from abuses, including abuses committed by armed groups and private individuals.
- Sexual violence and other gender-related abuses constitute a form of persecution within the meaning of the 1951 Convention. No one should be returned to a country where he or she is likely to face torture or persecution.

Ending impunity?

Impunity for violence against women is a problem in all circumstances. But access to justice for women victims of human rights abuses in areas of armed conflict is particularly difficult. The reasons are mutually reinforcing, creating a virtually unbreakable web of impunity. They include the overall climate of indifference towards many forms of violence against women; the tacit acceptance of rape and other forms of sexual violence as an unavoidable part of war; threats and reprisals against those who reveal abuses; the existence of special national legislation which prevents prosecutions for crimes committed in war; and amnesty laws as part of peace-making "deals". Added to this is the unwillingness of governments to meet their obligations under international humanitarian law, notably universal jurisdiction. According to this principle any state can and should bring to justice those presumed responsible for torture, crimes against humanity, war crimes, and genocide, regardless of the place where the crimes were committed, the nationality of the person responsible and the nationality of the victim. All states also have the obligation to cooperate in the detection, arrest, extradition and punishment of people implicated in these crimes.

The belief that torture of women is an unavoidable part of war has been challenged by women's organizations around the world. That challenge has gained new momentum following proceedings in the International Criminal Tribunals for the former Yugoslavia and Rwanda (Yugoslavia and Rwanda Tribunals). For instance, the Yugoslavia Tribunal has issued an indictment against eight men, several of whom are alleged to have repeatedly raped two Bosnian Muslim women who were detained and systematically raped for more than six months. This is the first trial at the Yugoslavia Tribunal in which rape and sexual enslavement has been treated as a crime against humanity. Both the Yugoslavia and Rwanda Tribunals have filed charges based on sexual violence and rape as constituent parts of the crime of genocide. These charges have been brought against those accused of committing the acts as well as against their superiors. In its decision of 2 September 1998,[60] the Rwanda Tribunal found that numerous Tutsi women seeking refuge from the massacres were systematically raped by armed local militia. In its judgment, the Tribunal stressed that rape and sexual violence constitute genocide if committed with intent to destroy a particular group, and held that sexual violence was an "integral" part of the process of destruction of the Tutsi ethnic group.

The Rome Statute of the International Criminal Court has incorporated a gender perspective to ensure that women who are victims of the gravest crimes under international law have access to justice and that women play a role in the Court.[61] AI calls on states to ratify the Rome Statute and also to enact legislation permitting their courts to exercise universal jurisdiction over grave violations of international law.

Women in armed conflicts

- Acts of violence against women, including sexual violence, are prohibited under both international human rights law and humanitarian law which governs the conduct of war (the Geneva Conventions and their Additional Protocols).
- Under customary international law, many acts of violence against women committed by parties to a conflict (whether international or internal) constitute torture. These include rape and gang rape, abduction and sexual slavery, forced marriage, forced impregnation and forced maternity, sexual mutilation, indecent assault and many other forms of physical violence.
- Rape and other forms of sexual violence by combatants in the conduct of armed conflicts are now recognized as war crimes.
- As set out in the Rome Statute of the International Criminal Court, the crime of rape includes situations where the victim provides sex to avoid harm, to obtain the necessities of life, or for other reasons which have effectively deprived her of her ability to consent.
- When sexual violence is committed on a systematic basis or a large scale, or as part of a widespread or systematic attack directed against a civilian population, it is a crime against humanity.
- Torture of women in armed conflict constitutes a grave breach of the Geneva Conventions.
- Torture of women may constitute an element of genocide, as defined in the Convention on the Prevention and Punishment of the Crime of Genocide.
- Acts of violence against women amounting to torture, war crimes, crimes against humanity and genocide are subject to universal jurisdiction.

4: Recommendations

The patterns, methods, causes and consequences of the torture of women are decisively influenced by the victims' gender. In order to be effective, therefore, a plan of action to combat the torture of women has to be based on a perspective that takes into account gender issues.

Torture of women is a fundamental violation of human rights, condemned by the international community as an offence to human dignity and prohibited in all circumstances under international law. Yet it persists, daily and across the globe. Immediate steps are needed to confront and eradicate the torture of women.

AI calls on all governments to implement the following recommendations. It invites concerned individuals and organizations to join AI in its campaign to ensure that they do so. These recommendations are drawn from a range of sources. Some are found in international human rights standards including the UN Convention against Torture and the UN Convention on the Elimination of All Forms of Discrimination against Women. Some are drawn from examples of good practice already put in place by some governments. Most arise from the experiences of non-governmental organizations which make up the global women's movement, and who are at the forefront of exposing and addressing acts of violence against women as human rights violations.

AI believes that governments have the power to implement these recommendations. Most do not need a huge investment of resources, but they do require political will and the conviction that torture of women can no longer be allowed to continue. AI believes that the implementation of these measures would be a positive indication of a government's commitment to end torture of women and to work for the eradication of violence against women worldwide.

However, these measures will not eradicate the torture of women unless discrimination on grounds of gender is addressed. In this, AI believes that everyone has a part to play — governments, political parties, religious groups, all elements of civil society and individuals. Everyone has a responsibility to commit themselves to the equality of all human beings, irrespective of gender, age, social status, racial, national or ethnic origin or sexual orientation.

1. Condemn all acts of violence against women

- States should clearly and publicly condemn all acts of violence against women, whether committed by law enforcement officials or private individuals.
- States should develop policies and disseminate materials to promote women's safety in the home, in society, and in detention, and to raise awareness about violence against women. States should promote the equality of women and men.
- States should undertake legal literacy campaigns to inform men and women of women's legal rights and to educate them specifically about domestic violence.
- The authorities should collect up-to-date statistical data on the prevalence of violence against women in the family and the community, should make it publicly available and should disseminate it widely.

2. Prohibit acts of violence against women and establish adequate legal protection against such acts

- States should prohibit in law and establish adequate legal protection against all acts of violence against women whether committed by state officials or private individuals. These include acts which take place within the community or within the family, such as marital rape.
- Governments should periodically review, evaluate and revise their laws, codes and procedures, including immigration regulations, to ensure their effectiveness in eliminating violence against women. States should remove provisions that allow for or condone violence against women.
- Governments should recognize that discrimination against women both in law and in practice is a key contributory factor to the torture and ill-treatment of women. In order to combat torture, governments should periodically review, evaluate and revise their laws, codes and procedures to

ensure that they do not discriminate against women and to enhance their effectiveness in eliminating discrimination against women. States should remove provisions that allow for or condone discrimination against women.

- States should enact legislation prohibiting slavery, debt bondage and the buying and selling of people. States should ensure that their criminal laws and criminal justice system treat trafficked women as victims of human rights abuses and as potential witnesses, rather than as criminals.
- States should ratify without reservation and implement all relevant treaties, including the Convention on the Elimination of All Forms of Discrimination against Women, the International Covenant on Civil and Political Rights, the International Covenant on Economic, Social and Cultural Rights, the Convention against Torture and Other Cruel, Inhuman or Degrading Treatment or Punishment, the Convention on the Rights of the Child and the International Convention on the Elimination of All Forms of Racial Discrimination. States should ensure that these treaties are reflected in national legislation. States should implement the Declaration on the Elimination of Violence against Women.
- States should ratify the Optional Protocol to the Convention on the Elimination of All Forms of Discrimination against Women. The Optional Protocol provides for individual petitions and for inquiries into systematic violations of the Convention, providing an international remedy for women who have suffered human rights abuses.
- States should comply with the reporting requirements of the various human rights treaties and should ensure the inclusion of gender-specific information wherever relevant.
- States should ratify and comply with the International Labour Organisation (ILO) conventions on the rights of migrant workers so as to reduce violence against women migrant workers.
- Governments should ensure that no woman or girl is forcibly returned to a country where she risks being tortured, including where the state fails to protect against torture by non-state actors. The detention of asylum-seekers should

normally be avoided. Where detention is lawful, the authorities should ensure that asylum-seekers are not subjected to cruel, inhuman or degrading treatment.

3. Investigate all allegations of violence against women

- States must ensure that prompt, thorough and impartial investigations are conducted into all reports of violence against women, whether perpetrated by law enforcement officials, armed groups or private individuals.
- Clear guidelines must be issued to law enforcement agencies, stating that deterring women from reporting acts of violence will not be tolerated and insisting on the duties of law enforcement officials to investigate acts of violence against women, whether perpetrated within their family or community, or in custody or armed conflict.
- States must ensure that women who have suffered abuses are not subjected to further abuses in the process of seeking redress because of laws insensitive to gender considerations, because of enforcement practices or because of other interventions by state officials.
- States must ensure that law enforcement agencies do not discriminate against women from immigrant or minority communities who report abuses.
- States should define the powers of the police to respond to violence against women in written policy, in accordance with international standards. States should provide training to all police, both veterans and new recruits, to enable them to deal effectively with allegations of violence against women. An adequate number of women police officers should be recruited.
- States must develop investigative techniques which do not degrade women subjected to violence and which minimize intrusion, while maintaining standards for the collection of evidence.
- Women who allege to police that they have been sexually assaulted should be examined promptly by a specialist medico-legal practitioner, female whenever possible.
- States should appoint police investigating officers who

specialize in such cases, and who are given additional training in the issues surrounding violence against women and the use of medical and other forensic evidence.

4. Prosecute and punish

- States should remove immediately gender-discriminatory provisions which do not allow women to testify in court or do not give full weight to women's testimony.
- States should undertake a study of conviction rates in respect of crimes of violence perpetrated against women, in order to evaluate whether the existing legal and judicial system discriminates against victims of abuses who are women.
- States should undertake a comprehensive review of the current legal framework relating to crimes of violence against women to ensure its effectiveness in the prosecution of acts of violence against women.
- States should provide specific training to all judges and lawyers to enhance understanding of violence against women, its causes and consequences. An adequate number of women judges should be appointed.
- Courts at all levels should identify specialized prosecutors to handle cases of sexual abuse and rape, who should receive additional training in the issues surrounding gender violence.

5. Provide adequate remedies and ensure reparation

- States should establish special units or procedures in hospitals to help identify women victims of violence and to provide them with medical care and counselling.
- States should provide a mechanism through which victim-survivors can obtain state protection, and should ensure rigorous enforcement of measures such as protection orders.
- A national directory of governmental and non-governmental services available to women victims of violence should be developed, and information should be distributed to police stations and local courts, as well as to district surgeons, hospitals and other health care facilities. Information about local referral services for women victims of violence should

be made available in several languages to ensure that women from all communities are made aware of their rights.
- Women who have been subjected to violence should be provided with information on their rights and on how to obtain remedies, in addition to information about participating in criminal proceedings.
- States should provide emergency services to women victims of violence. These could include crisis intervention services; transportation from the victim's home to a medical centre, shelter or safe haven; immediate medical attention; emergency legal advice and referral; crisis counselling; financial assistance; childcare support; and specific services for women of minority or immigrant communities.
- Victims of violence and their dependants should be entitled to obtain prompt reparation, including compensation, medical care and rehabilitation.

6. Protection against torture in custody
- Governments must publicly recognize that rape and sexual abuse of women in custody always constitute torture or ill-treatment and will not be tolerated. Sexual abuse includes threats, virginity testing, fondling, and the deliberate use of body searches or sexually explicit language to degrade or humiliate.
- Military, police and prison personnel must be explicitly informed that anyone who commits such human rights violations will be promptly brought to justice, and if convicted will face penalties commensurate with the seriousness of the crime. (Such penalties must, however, exclude corporal punishment and the death penalty.)
- Female detainees and prisoners must be held separately from male detainees and prisoners, and must not share bathing or toilet facilities (in accordance with UN Standard Minimum Rules for the Treatment of Prisoners, rule 8(a)). The non-compliance of prison officials with rules such as the separation of women and men in prison is tantamount to acquiescence in violence against women detainees.
- In line with UN Standard Minimum Rule 53, female security

personnel should be present during the interrogation of women detainees and should be solely responsible for conducting body searches of women detainees. There should be no contact between male guards and female prisoners without the presence of a female guard.

- The imprisonment of a mother and child together must never be used to inflict torture or ill-treatment on either by causing physical or mental suffering. If a child is separated from its mother in prison, the mother should be immediately notified and kept continuously informed of the child's whereabouts. She should be given reasonable access to the child.
- Any female detainee or prisoner who alleges that she has been raped or sexually abused must be given an immediate medical examination, preferably by a female doctor, or at least in the presence of female personnel.
- Victims of rape and sexual abuse and other torture and ill-treatment in custody should be entitled to fair prompt, and adequate reparation, including compensation and all appropriate medical care.
- The practice of incommunicado detention should be ended. Governments should ensure that all prisoners are brought before an independent judicial authority without delay after being taken into custody. Prisoners should have access to relatives, lawyers and doctors without delay and regularly thereafter.
- Governments should ensure that prisoners are held only in officially recognized places of detention and that accurate information about their arrest and whereabouts is made available immediately to relatives, lawyers and the courts. Effective judicial remedies should be available to enable relatives and lawyers to find out immediately where a prisoner is held and under what authority and to ensure the prisoner's safety.
- All prisoners should be immediately informed of their rights. These include the right to lodge complaints about their treatment and to have a judge rule without delay on the lawfulness of their detention. Judges should investigate any

evidence of torture and order release if the detention is unlawful. A lawyer should be present during interrogations. Governments should ensure that conditions of detention conform to international standards for the treatment of prisoners and take into account the special needs of women. The authorities responsible for detention should be separate from those in charge of interrogation. There should be regular, independent, unannounced and unrestricted visits of inspection to all places of detention.
- Governments should ensure that statements and other evidence obtained through torture may not be invoked in any proceedings, except against a person accused of torture.

7. Prevention of torture of women in armed conflicts

- States should implement gender-sensitive human rights and humanitarian law training for all army personnel and personnel involved in UN or regional peace-keeping and humanitarian aid. States should launch public awareness campaigns on the torture of women in armed conflicts which stress that acts of violence against women, including sexual violence, are prohibited under both international human rights law and humanitarian law. Many such acts constitute torture or cruel, inhuman or degrading treatment. They also may constitute war crimes, crimes against humanity, and an element of genocide.
- Parties to a conflict, including armed opposition groups, should issue clear orders that torture, including rape and other sexual abuse of women and girls, will not be tolerated under any circumstances.
- Donor countries, humanitarian agencies and national governments should fund and adopt gender-sensitive assistance programs for women victims of violence.
- Codes of conduct and guidelines to ensure that humanitarian assistance is gender-sensitive and does not discriminate against women should be adopted by all agencies involved in humanitarian programs. In particular, women victims of violence should be given access to health care and counselling. Women must be given a voice in the design and

implementation of assistance programs.
- States should ratify immediately Additional Protocols I and II to the Geneva Conventions of 1949.
- States should ratify immediately the Rome Statute of the International Criminal Court (ICC) and ensure that their national legislation is in line with the ICC's requirements.
- States should implement the principle of universal jurisdiction. According to this principle any state can and should bring to justice those presumed responsible for torture, crimes against humanity, war crimes, and genocide, regardless of the place where the crimes were committed, the nationality of the person responsible and the nationality of the victim. All states also have the obligation to cooperate in the detection, arrest, extradition and punishment of people implicated in these crimes.
- States should implement a gender-sensitive approach to refugee determination procedures and refugee protection. International protection should be given to those whom their own state is unwilling or unable to protect from abuses, including abuses committed by armed groups and private individuals.

8. Human rights defenders

- States should recognize the valuable contribution made by human rights activists, lawyers and women's rights groups in raising awareness of women's rights and combating abuses.
- States should ensure that human rights defenders and human rights groups can pursue their legitimate activities without harassment, or fear for their own or their families' safety. States should provide adequate police protection to public and private shelters run for women, as well as to human rights defenders exposed to threats or harassment, and should pursue all such threats with a view to punishment. Governmental and non-governmental services should be adequately funded.
- States should ensure that the principles contained in the Declaration on the Right and Responsibility of Individuals,

Groups and Organs of Society to Promote and Protect Universally Recognized Human Rights and Fundamental Freedoms, adopted by the UN General Assembly in 1998, are incorporated into national law and implemented in practice.

9. Intergovernmental bodies

- The UN's procedures and mechanisms aimed at fighting torture, in particular the Committee against Torture, should address specifically abuses committed against women, including torture of women at the hands of private perpetrators.
- The intergovernmental bodies which address the issue of torture should ensure that their work is gender-sensitive. An increasing number of the experts who participate in these bodies should be women. All those involved in such work should receive gender-sensitive training. All UN and other intergovernmental bodies working to combat torture should revise their working methods to incorporate a comprehensive gender analysis.
- UN and other intergovernmental bodies working on the issue of torture should identify, collect and use gender-specific data and apply gender analysis to monitoring and reporting.

ENDNOTES

1 The Declaration on the Elimination of Violence against Women defines such violence as "any act of gender-based violence that results in, or is likely to result in, physical, sexual, or psychological harm or suffering to women, including threats of such acts, coercion or arbitrary deprivation of liberty, whether occurring in public or private life". It includes "violence perpetrated or condoned by the State, wherever it occurs" and "violence occurring in the family" and the "general community".

2 AI is impartial in its reporting of human rights abuses, and strives to achieve global coverage. In this report, which focuses on a new area of work for AI, the examples cited reflect the areas where AI has pursued this new area, and are therefore weighted towards South Asia. AI's recent published work on abuses by private individuals has included: *Pakistan: Honour killings of girls and women* (AI Index: ASA 33/18/99); *Female Genital Mutilation: A Human Rights Information Pack* (AI Index: ACT 77/05/97); and *Israel: Human rights abuses of women trafficked from countries of the former Soviet Union into Israel's sex industry* (AI Index: MDE 15/17/00).

3 *Respect, Protect, Fulfill: Women's Human Rights — State responsibility for abuses by 'non-state actors'* (AI Index: IOR 50/001/2000)

4 General Comment No. 20 on Article 7 of the International Covenant on Civil and Political Rights.

5 Case of *A v. United Kingdom* (application 25599/94), Judgment of 23 September 1998.

6 "Even the special attribution rule contained in Article 1 of the Torture Convention, limiting torture to conduct of state officials, is capable of a more flexible interpretation than was envisaged by the framers." J. Crawford, UN International Law Commission Special Rapporteur on State Responsibility, "Revising the Draft Article on State Responsibility", 10 European Journal of International Law, 435-46 (1999), p.440.

7 UN Doc. E/CN.4/1996/53, para.32.

8 *Velásquez Rodríguez v. Honduras*, (ser.C.) No.4, Judgment of 29 July 1988, para.172.

9 Ibid, para. 174.

10 Wanja N. Githinji was awarded the CNN Journalist of the Year Award in April 2000.

11 AFP, 5 June 2000.

12 UN Doc. E/CN.4/2000/68, paras 54-60.

13 *Ending Violence Against Women*, based on over 50 population surveys, was published by the Johns Hopkins University Population Information Program, USA, in early 2000.

14 "Scream quietly, or the neighbours will hear", *Indian Express*, 29 August 2000.

15 UNICEF, *Domestic Violence Against Women and Girls*, May 2000.

16 *Saudi Arabia: Gross human rights abuses against women*, (AI Index: MDE 23/57/00).

17 KALAYAAN, a campaigning organization for domestic workers.

18 Recognition that forced marriage is a practice similar to slavery may be found in an international treaty, the Supplementary Convention on the Abolition of Slavery, the Slave Trade and Institutions and Practices Similar to Slavery, 1956.

19 Change, *Non-Consensual Sex in Marriage: A worldwide programme*, London: UK, November 2000.

20 See: *Pakistan: Violence against women in the name of honour*, (AI Index: ASA 33/17/99).

21 For a detailed study of legal issues involved in the abduction of South Asian women for the purpose of forced marriage see: *Submission by the International Centre for the Legal Protection of Human Rights (INTERIGHTS), Ain O Salish Kendra (ASK) and Shirkat Gah to the Home Office Working Group: Information Gathering Exercise on Forced Marriages*, March 2000.

22 Attiya Dawood, "Karo-kari: A question of honour, but whose honour?", *Feminista*, 2(3/4), April 1999.

23 AFP, 10 May 2000.

24 Slavery is defined in the Slavery Convention of 1926 as "the status or condition of a person over whom any or all the powers attaching to the right of ownership are exercised".

25 UN Doc. E/CN.4/1997/47, 12 February 1997.

26 UN Doc. E/CN.4/SUB.2/Res/2000/10, para. 2, 17 August 2000.

27 Helen Kijo-Bisimba of the Legal Human Rights Centre, Dar es Salam, Panafrican News Agency, 12 August 2000.

28 Ruth Evans: "Cutting out a tradition in Mali", BBC News, 21 August 2000.

29 Beijing Declaration and Platform for Action, UN Doc. A/CONF.177/20(1995), paras. 124-130.

30 UN Doc. E/CN.4/1996/53, para 141.

31 UN Doc. E/CN.4/2000/68, para 53.

32 UN Doc. E/CN.4/1997/47.

33 Change, *Non-Consensual Sex in Marriage: A worldwide programme*, London: UK, November 2000. The final results of the survey were not yet available at the time of writing.

34 The UN Special Rapporteur on violence against women has emphasized the role of official anti-immigration policies in casting victims of trafficking as culprits and the equation by many governments of illegal migration and trafficking. E/CN.4/2000/68 paras 43-46.

35 See UN Special Rapporteur on violence against women, UN Doc. E/CN.4/2000/68, executive summary. The new Protocol to the UN Convention against Transnational Organized Crime (see above) contains a useful definition of trafficking in Article 3a.

36 UN Doc. E/CN.4/2000/68, para 45.

37 UN. Doc. CCPR/C/79/Add.93, Concluding Observations/Comments, adopted on 28 July 1998, para 16.

38 UN Doc. E/CN.4/2000/68, paras 61- 65.

39 Under section 155(4) of the Indian Evidence Act.

40 Under section 54(1) of the Indian Evidence Act.

41 Dr Rebecca Malepe, a local human rights activist in Swaziland.

42 World Bank funded study, AFP, 9 May 2000.

43 *Saudi Arabia: Gross human rights abuses against women*, (AI Index: MDE 23/57/00).

44 Interights, above note 21, page 30.

45 *Re KR*, 1999 [2] FLR 542.

46 A total of 20 paid staff work for these two hotlines. See République française, *Rapport sur la mise en oeuvre par la France des recommendations du programme d'action de la quatrième conférence mondiale sur les femmes: Pékin Plus Cinq*, octobre 1999. These figures do not include the provision of services by local authorities.

47 AFP, 7 July 2000.

48 *Beyond Victims and Villains, The culture of sexual violence in South Johannesburg*, a study conducted by CIET Africa and the Johannesburg Southern Metropolitan Local Council of Greater Johannesburg, presented in June 2000.

49 "Effective check on trafficking of women urged", *Dawn*, Karachi, 6 May 2000.

50 AI and International Centre for Human Rights and Democratic Development (ICHRDD), *Documenting Human Rights Violations by State Agents: Sexual Violence*, Montreal: ICHRDD, 1999.

51 *Saudi Arabia: Gross human rights abuses against women*, (AI Index: MDE 23/57/00).

52 *USA (Texas) - Allegations of Cruel and Degrading Punishment Against Women*, (AI Index: AMR 51/90/00).

53 See for instance, Report to the UN Commission on Human Rights, 12 January 1995, UN Doc. E/CN.4/1995/34, para.189.

54 Inter-American Commission on Human Rights, Report No 5/96, *Fernando and Raquel Mejía v. Peru* (1 March 1996). In its decision, the Inter-American Commission on Human Rights found that rape of a woman at her home by a security official amounted to torture under Article 5 of the American Convention on Human Rights. The Inter-American Commission noted that rape by a state official meets each of the three necessary components of torture under contemporary international law.

55 Standard Minimum Rules for the Treatment of Prisoners (1977): Article 8 provides for the separation of the different categories of prisoners according to their sex, age, criminal record and other considerations. Additionally, Article 9 (1) prescribes that "... it is not desirable to have two prisoners in a cell or room".

56 For further information see *Sierra Leone: Rape and other forms of sexual violence against girls and women* (AI Index: AFR 51/35/00).

57 See for instance, *Sexual violence against refugees, Guidelines on prevention and response*. Geneva, United Nations High Commissioner for Refugees, 1995.

58 See for example: *Quintero v. Uruguay*, Communication No. 107/1981, Reports of the Human Rights Committee; Concluding Observations of the Human Rights Committee: Algeria, UN Doc. CCPR/C/79/Add.95 (18/8/98), para 10; UN Doc. E/CN.4/1983/14, para 13; *Velásquez Rodríguez Case*, Inter-American Court of Human Rights, 29 July 1988, paras 155-6; *Blake Case*, Inter-American Court of Human Rights, 24 January 1998, para 97; *Kurt v. Turkey*, Judgment of the European Court of Human Rights (25 May 1998) para 134.

59 United Nations High Commissioner for Refugees, *Guidelines on the Protection of Refugee Women*, Geneva, July 1991, p.34.

60 ICTR, Decision of 2 September 1998; *The Prosecutor v. Jean-Paul Akayesu; Case No. ICTR-96-4-T*. Jean Paul Akayesu was sentenced to life imprisonment in October 1998.

61 *The International Criminal Court: Fact sheet 7 - Ensuring justice for women* (AI Index: IOR 40/08/00).

WHAT YOU CAN DO

- Join our campaign — **Take a step to stamp out torture.** You can help stamp out torture. Add your voice to Amnesty International's campaign. Help us to make a difference. Contact your national office of Amnesty International and ask for information about how to join the campaign, including information on how to take action on some of the specific cases featured in this report.
- Become a member of Amnesty International and other local and international human rights organizations which fight torture.
- Make a donation to support Amnesty International's work.
- Tell friends and family about the campaign and ask them to join too.

Campaigning Online

The website **www.stoptorture.org** allows visitors to access Amnesty International's information about torture. It will also offer the opportunity to appeal on behalf of individuals at risk of being tortured. Those registering onto the site will receive urgent e-mail messages alerting them to take action during the campaign.

- Register to take action against torture at **www.stoptorture.org**

☐ I would like to join your campaign. Please send me more information.
☐ I would like to join Amnesty International. Please send me details.
☐ I would like to donate to Amnesty International's campaign to stamp out torture.

Credit card number: ☐☐☐☐ ☐☐☐☐ ☐☐☐☐ ☐☐☐☐

Expiry date ———— / ———— £ ———— [amount]

Signature ————

Name ————

Address ————

Please photocopy this coupon and send it to:
Amnesty International, International Secretariat, Campaign against Torture,
1 Easton Street, London WC1X 0DW, United Kingdom